FIFTEEN DAYS OF PRAYER

Visit our web site at
www.albahouse.org
(for orders www.stpauls.us)

or call 1-800-343-2522 (ALBA)
and request current catalog

Fifteen Days of Prayer with Father Marie-Eugène of the Child Jesus, Carmelite

Founder of Notre-Dame de Vie

Roselyne Deglaire and Joëlle Guichard

Translated by Teresa Hawes

Library of Congress Cataloging-in-Publication Data

Deglaire, Roselyne.
  [Prier 15 jours avec le Père Marie-Eugène. English]
  Fifteen days of prayer with Marie-Eugène of the Child Jesus : Carmelite, founder of Notre-Dame de vie / by Roselyne Deglaire and Joëlle Guichard ; translated by Teresa Hawes.
     p. cm.
  ISBN 978-0-8189-1276-4
  1. Marie-Eugène de l'Enfant-Jésus, père, 1894-1967—Meditations. 2. Spiritual life—Catholic Church. I. Guichard, Joëlle. II. Title.
  BX4705.M3855.D4413 2009
  269'.6—dc22

2009009498

Produced and designed in the United States of America by the
Fathers and Brothers of the Society of St. Paul,
2187 Victory Boulevard, Staten Island, New York 10314-6603
as part of their communications apostolate.

ISBN-10: 0-8189-1276-6
ISBN-13: 978-0-8189-1276-4

© Copyright 2009 by the Society of St. Paul / Alba House

Printing Information:

Current Printing - first digit   1 2 3 4 5 6 7 8 9 10

Year of Current Printing - first year shown

2009 2010 2011 2012 2013 2014 2015 2016 2017 2018

TABLE OF CONTENTS

List of Abbreviations vii
Surrendered to God's Grace ix
Itinerary xix
1. At the Wellsprings of Prayer 1
2. A Mysterious Likeness 9
3. Where is He? 17
4. Praying with my Whole Being 25
5. Have Faith in Your Faith 31
6. Safe in Darkness 39
7. The Holy Spirit, our Friend, Is Here 47
8. The Price of Freedom 55
9. In the Humdrum of Ordinary Life 61
10. Birds' Wings 67
11. Trusting to the Point of Audacity 73
12. Come Day, Come Night 79
13. Christ Belongs Entirely To Us 85
14. Servant of the Kingdom, Sent by the Spirit 93
15. Mary, Faithful to the Love that Took Possession of Her 99

LIST OF ABBREVIATIONS

FATHER MARIE-EUGÈNE OF THE CHILD JESUS

- UD   Unpublished documents (lectures, homilies, personal notes).
- UTL   *Under the Torrent of His Love, Thérèse of Lisieux, a Spiritual Genius*; trans.: Sr. Mary Thomas Noble, OP. New York: ST PAULS/Alba House, 1995.
- WSB   *Where the Spirit Breathes, Prayer and Action*; trans.: Sr. Mary Thomas Noble, OP. New York: ST PAULS/Alba House, 1998.
- C-88   Revue *Carmel* 1988/3-4, #51 – Numéro spécial: *Un maître spirituel, le père Marie-Eugène o.c.d.*
- CR   *Croyez à la folie de l'amour qui est en Dieu.* Toulouse: Éditions du Carmel, 2004.
- M   Règue, Raymonde. *Père Marie-Eugène de l'Enfant Jésus, maître spirituel pour notre temps.* Venasque: Éditions du Carmel, 1978.
- PM   *Père d'une multitude, Lettres autobiographiques.* Paris: Fayard, Le Sarment, 1988.
- P   *Jean de la Croix, Présence de Lumière.* Venasque: Éditions du Carmel, 1991.
- PP   *Les Premiers Pas de l'Enfant Dieu.* Toulouse: Éditions du Carmel, 2001.
- JVVD   *Je Veux Voir Dieu.* Tarascon: Éditions du Carmel, 1956.
- VM   *La Vierge Marie toute Mère*, 3e éd. Toulouse: Éditions du Carmel, 2001.

TERESA OF AVILA

- IC   *The Interior Castle.*
  The Collected Works of St. Teresa of Avila, Volume

> II; trans.: Kieran Kavanaugh, O.C.D. and Otilio Rodriguez, O.C.D. Washington, DC: ICS Publications, 1980.

L   *The Book of Her Life.*
> *The Collected Works of St. Teresa of Avila*, Volume I, 2nd edition (Revised); trans.: Kieran Kavanaugh, O.C.D. and Otilio Rodriquez, O.C.D. Washington, DC: ICS Publications, 1987.

WP   *The Way of Perfection.*
> *The Collected Works of St. Teresa of Avila*, Volume II; trans.: Kieran Kavanaugh, O.C.D. and Otilio Rodriguez, O.C.D. Washington, DC: ICS Publications, 1980.

JOHN OF THE CROSS

AMC   *The Ascent of Mount Carmel.*
> *The Collected Works of St. John of the Cross*, Revised Edition; trans.: Kieran Kavanaugh, O.C.D. and Otilio Rodriguez, O.C.D. Washington, DC: ICS Publications, 1991.

DN   *The Dark Night*, ibid.

LF   *The Living Flame of Love*, ibid.

THÉRÈSE OF LISIEUX

LC   *Her Last Conversations*, trans.: John Clarke, O.C.D. Washington, DC: ICS Publications, 1977.

LT   *Letters of St. Thérèse of Lisieux*, Volume II, trans.: John Clarke, O.C.D. Washington, DC: ICS Publications, 1988.

Ms   *The Story of a Soul, The Autobiography of Saint Thérèse of Lisieux*, 3rd edition; trans.: John Clarke, O.C.D. Washington, DC: ICS Publications, 1996.

NB: The biblical abbreviations follow those given in the *New American Bible*, 2004–2005 edition. Wichita, KS: Devore and Sons, Inc., 1987.

SURRENDERED TO GOD'S GRACE
(1894-1967)

Speaking of the Holy Spirit, Father Marie-Eugène used to say: *"Before enlightening your heart, the Holy Spirit sheds light through events and situations... light in darkness; you don't know where it's going, you don't know where it's coming from"* (1965); then, quite simply: *"I call Him my friend and I believe I have reasons for doing so"* and also: *"The Holy Spirit has always foiled my projects, but for the better."*

These words express an intimate experience of the Holy Spirit's presence. Taking a look at Father Marie-Eugène's life implies discovering this active presence of the Spirit of Love who chose him for a mission: to lead men and women to divine intimacy, the aim of any Christian life.

Henri Grialou was born on December 2nd, 1894, in Le Gua, a town in the Decazeville mining region of Aveyron, southwestern France. He was the third of five children. His father was a miner who died unexpectedly in 1904; Henri was not yet ten. The family then experienced the hardships of poverty and Mrs. Grialou had to work hard to raise her five children. But they were nurtured by the priceless treasure of their mother's abundant love and strong faith. This was particularly true of young Henri.

Very early on his child's heart heard the call to the priesthood. His valiant mother managed to assume the cost of his studies by accepting a great deal of sacrifice.

In the seminary, Henri was a bright student and an excellent classmate, *everybody's friend*: all the testimonies highlight this. During these seminary years he discovered Thérèse of the Child Jesus – *a childhood friend*, as he would say – whose message he would penetrate more deeply with an ever-renewed joy.

1914: war broke out. As an officer, Henri participated in the most important battles; he learned how to be a leader, and encountered suffering and death on a daily basis. War was a tough school. Demobilized in 1919, matured by the trial of four years of combat, inhabited by an intense desire for prayer and silence, he chose to return to the seminary: *"I made a definitive choice to become a priest."*

On December 13th, 1920, an imperious and overwhelming call committed his life once and for all. That evening, Henri read *The Abridged Life of John of the Cross*. When he closed the book, an absolute, irresistible certainty took hold of him: God wanted him to join the Discalced Carmelite Order. He knew nothing about their way of life; he had never seen a Carmelite friar and… he wondered whether he had lost his mind. To carry out this imperative vocation, Henri would then run up against violent opposition including the most unexpected, the most painful: his mother's.

Ordained a priest on February 4th, 1922, on the 24th he entered the Carmelite friars' novitiate in Avon, south of Paris. He had then sacrificed everything, leaving prostrate his mother, whose suffering deeply affected him. In the austerity of novitiate life, Brother Marie-Eugène of the Child Jesus discovered the very depths of Carmel's grace. In the light of Teresa of Avila and John of the Cross, he most especially discovered the grace of silent prayer, which abundantly quenched his inner thirst. He would remain unfailingly faithful to it his whole life long, and would continually teach its paths. This was a time of intense purification, and also a time of profound graces when the Holy Spirit let him catch a glimpse of his mission and sense his spiritual fatherhood.

In 1923, the beatification of Thérèse of Lisieux was an immense joy for him. Since he understood the depth of *the little saint's spiritual genius*, he spoke of *immense hopes for the future.*

From the very beginning of his ministry in the northern French city of Lille he was placed in charge of the journal *Carmel*. He realized that people were waiting for Carmelite doctrine in places far beyond the monasteries. From then on he bore within himself the desire to see contemplation spread through *the highways and byways of the world.*

1928 brought an unexpected change: he was named Superior of the Petit Castelet monastery at Tarascon, near Avignon.

Now as it happened, on the feast of Pentecost, 1929, three young ladies came to see him. They were teachers and co-principals of a secondary school for girls in Marseille called Cours Notre-Dame de France. Wanting to consecrate themselves to God, attracted by Carmelite spirituality, they came to ask this young friar, already known for his spiritual discernment, for advice. They were to become the foundation stones of Notre-Dame de Vie Institute; one of them, Marie Pila, would be its co-foundress.

An astonishing spiritual adventure then began in 1932 at Notre-Dame de Vie, a piece of property providentially given to Father Marie-Eugène. No one really knew what form this adventure would take, all the more so as more than once puzzling events seemed to *block* the road to any plan.

Indeed, successive appointments within the Carmelite Order led Father Marie-Eugène from the Petit Castelet all the way to Rome, taking him far from Notre-Dame de Vie. Elected General Definitor in 1937, he had to reside in Rome, while at the same time his Superior enjoined him to take care of the budding foundation, *God's creation* as he was told. As a matter of fact, at Notre-Dame de Vie, vocations were coming and the small group slowly grew, in darkness, very often in an unpredictable way, according to the Spirit's breath and under the watchful care of Mary, Mother of Life.

1939 brought war once again. The general mobilization called Marie-Eugène back to

France. Demobilized as early as 1940, he could not return to Rome because of the hostilities. In the midst of the time's uncertainties and dangers, he continued his mission as a preacher, never sacrificing the demands of his contemplative life to his intense apostolic life. *"My life remains calm, deep and recollected as is any life in Carmel."* His entire apostolic ardor flowed from his faithfulness to silent prayer.

In 1946 he went back to Rome to the central government of the Discalced Carmelite Friars. In 1948, the Pope named him apostolic Visitor of the Carmelite nuns' monasteries in France, and made him responsible for organizing the Carmelite nuns into federations. At the same time, Father Marie-Eugène paternally kept watch over the Notre-Dame de Vie foundation which was blossoming.

At the time when he was giving his all in the service of the Carmelite Order, Notre-Dame de Vie was officially recognized as a Secular Institute. Thus was Father Marie-Eugène able to see how well this new framework for the consecrated life, instituted by the Church, corresponded to his deepest spiritual intuitions.

Actively involved in professional life, the

members of Notre-Dame de Vie Institute live out the demands of the Carmelite spirit in the midst of the world: Give witness to the Living God! *On the highways and byways*, they share the lives of those whose thirst for God has very often been left asleep, though still alive, by the conditions of their lives. The strength that is necessary for Notre-Dame de Vie members to live out this ideal is rooted, after two years of initial formation, in praying silently for two hours each day and in returning on a regular basis to the *houses of solitude*. These visits are at once times of desert, renewal and community life.

Meanwhile, in Rome, Father Marie-Eugène was putting the finishing touches on his masterpiece, *I Want to See God / I am a Daughter of the Church*, the fruit of thirty years of spiritual experience. The book, a synthesis of Carmelite doctrine whose backbone is silent prayer, was published in 1949. It has continued to be in demand worldwide since then.

In 1954, when the Father General died unexpectedly, Marie-Eugène had to assume his function for the interim. Responsible for the entire Carmelite Order, he undertook a visit to the Middle and Far East monasteries. Some of these were then coming up against Marxist ideology. His gaze turned toward the immensity of China, he took part in the sufferings of the Church who was living her Lord's passion. He came back from that trip deeply marked by some of the people he had met, as his letters indicate.

In 1954 as well, the Institute was implanted in the Philippines. Writing to the woman who was responsible for the foundation, he exclaimed: *"Remember that Notre-Dame de Vie needs to witness to the Living God, to the Spirit of Love, not to a specific civilization."*

In 1955, Father Marie-Eugène returned to France. There he continued, as the founder of Notre-Dame de Vie Institute and as the Provincial of the Carmelite Friars of Avignon-Aquitaine, to work on the scale of the universal Church.

At that time, the Institute was rapidly spreading all over the world: after the Philippines, there were Germany, Mexico, Spain, Canada, Poland, and Japan. But he enlarged the space of his "tent" considerably: a priests' branch and a consecrated laymen's branch in turn took shape, approved by the Church in 1960 and 1963 respectively. Associate members and couples also came to live the same spirit. As Marie-Eugène would say: *"It's the Holy Spirit and Our Blessed Mother who have done everything here."*

Far from surprising him, the Second Vatican Council filled him with enthusiasm. He could not wait to make its decrees known and have them studied.

Falling ill, he watched his strength decline little by little. On Easter Sunday, 1967, overcome by suffering, profoundly adhering to and united with the Spirit of Love who was irresistibly calling him, he left his children this last will and testament: *"Remain faithful to the spirit of the Institute: action and contemplation closely united."* Then he murmured: *"As for me, I am on my way to perfect union with the Holy Spirit."* He died the following day, March 27th, Easter Monday, the feast day he had established in honor of Mary, Mother of the Risen One, Mother of Life.

ITINERARY

On April 24th, 2005, from Saint Peter's Square, Benedict XVI reminded all of us: "Each of us is the result of a thought of God. Each of us is willed, each of us is loved, each of us is necessary. There is nothing more beautiful than to be surprised by the Gospel, by the encounter with Christ."

How can we let Christ journey with us? How can we respond to His love? By praying, Father Marie-Eugène answers. In this little book he will lead us on this path to a living relationship and union with God. We are all called to this: a path of holiness, God's life in us, baptismal grace.... Here Marie-Eugène shares with us the fruit of his personal experience but also his response to a specific call from men and women who are searching for God, asking to be enlightened on their way that is not always easy to find in the dark.

The first three days invite us to take this

truth seriously: prayer is God's gift to each and every one of us.

[1st day] Someone, God, has been waiting for me forever. Someone, God, the hidden God, lets me seek Him and gives me the ability to find Him freely, personally. He gives me the ability to meet Him, know Him and love Him. These may be "formulas" that we constantly use without really paying attention to them. What do they mean?

[2nd day] God comes to me in Jesus, His Son; grace makes me God's child in Christ. We enter prayer, a dialogue with God, not "by our own strength but by letting grace take us by the hand," said John Paul II.

[3rd day] Where is God? He is within me, alive and active. He calls me and gives me the ability to go to Him. God's gift to me is God Himself. The spiritual life is a "progressive interiorization" toward this God who lives within me.

The following days [4th to 12th days] invite us to consider that prayer is also my gift to God, my response to God's love, a personal journey toward God. And God gives me the ability to reach Him in truth.

[4th day] In prayer I go to God with my

whole being. I strive with all that I am toward God's presence within me.

[5th and 6th days] But my encounter with God often leaves me puzzled; this presence I am striving toward remains dark and invisible, even though it is real and active. That's when I need to understand the essential and incomparable role of faith.

[7th day] And God comes to meet me. The Holy Spirit is within me. He comes to perfect my prayer, enlighten what I do. Jesus' promise is thus fulfilled.

[8th day] In the reciprocity of love, my gift to God gradually becomes a permanent disposition. This disposition gains meaning and value in light of Christ's offering to His Father, for God's joy and for His ongoing creation.

[9th day] My Christian life develops under God's gaze, united to Him, in the midst of my daily routine, where I am called to holiness.

[10th and 11th days] Along with faith, there is hope that leads me to God. Hope brings me to where I look to God for everything with absolute trust because in my spiritual life, I so quickly experience my own weakness. On the journey of prayer, hope is "in crisis" when I experience my own poverty. This becomes a luminous experience of the folly of God's merciful love.

[12th day] And little by little, throughout the days' darkness, *"the slow, deep work of grace"* follows its course, as Father Marie-Eugène assures us. This happens almost without my knowing it.

God loves me; He gives me the ability to love Him; and in giving me the ability to love Him, He gives me the ability to love others. Prayer, God's gift to each and every one of us, and our gift to God, is also a mission [13th to 15th days].

[13th and 14th days] United to Christ, I am called to participate in His mystery. The Holy Spirit, fulfilling and prolonging Christ's mission, takes me as part of His ongoing creation, the Church.

[15th day] And in the shifting phases of my prayer, Mary is present, as she was and as she always is, close to her Son. I discover her, Mother of Mercy close to me, her child, and I pray with her.

FIRST DAY

AT THE WELLSPRINGS OF PRAYER

God is Love. He created us out of love. He redeemed us out of love, and has destined us to a very close union with Him. This union fulfills God's most cherished desires. God-Love needs to give Himself and finds His joy in this, a joy according to the measure of His giving.

How great, then, will be God's joy when He finds a soul that leaves Him entirely free, and in whom He can pour out His love as much as He wants to! The secrets shared by Our Lord let us catch a glimpse of God's joy: "There will be more joy in Heaven over the conversion of a sinner…."

The meeting of our love with God-Love, the affectionate exchange that is immediately established: that is silent prayer. (JVVD 57–58; 37)[1]

---

[1] References to *I Want to See God / I am a Daughter of the Church*, trans.: Sr. M. Verda Claire, C.S.C. (Chicago: Fides Publishers, 1951/1953) indicate the single volume French work: *Je Veux Voir Dieu* (Tarascon: Éditions du Carmel, 1956). Passages may have been slightly modified to fit the context.

"God is Love."

Let's stop for a moment.

Beyond all the things we have to do which, minute by minute, eat us up and pull us away from ourselves, or the darkness that sometimes weighs us down like a lead cloak, let's enter deep within ourselves, like someone who has rediscovered the Love that makes us live, or like the prodigal son in the Gospel who comes back after a life of adventure, or else like Zacchaeus, "who wanted to see Jesus". Let's rediscover Him deep within ourselves, within the root of our very existence; this existence which we have received, which is a gift. Within this life, sometimes disconcerting and mysterious, let's welcome Jesus' words: "I want to stay at your house; I want to live within you." Beyond our forgetfulness, our denials, our wounds, let's rediscover who we really are; let's descend into the ever-living depths, where hope breathes, and there, let's listen to God's word: "Even before I formed you in your mother's womb, I knew you for my own"; "you are priceless in my eyes and I love you" (Jr 1:5; Is 43:4).

God is Love, John the Evangelist testifies.

God is Love! Marie-Eugène reiterates this

with all the saints. What a treasure we do indeed have in the Word of God that can neither deceive nor be deceived; a faithful Word that will not pass away; a Word that concurs with what we may not dare to hope for, an infinite Word that goes beyond what we can imagine or conceive. Father Marie-Eugène believed this. One of his contemporaries, Father Vercoustre, meeting him for the first time, jotted down: "I found myself before a man who took God seriously." His whole life was filled with the desire to lead people to discover God-Love. On this path he spoke from experience.

"With an eternal love, I love you." Is it true? Yes. Because God IS, and He is Love. How often, like the saints, did Marie-Eugène plunge into this eternal love, God Himself, into this love that is the wellspring of all God's acts within time: *Whether there be sunshine, fog or storm, we are always in God's mercy. Once mercy has taken hold of us, it never lets us go* (M 93). This is the power of Love that grasps, transforms, conquers and makes us act, the breath of creating and saving Love, the ultimate wellspring of our trust. Throughout the situations and events that shake the world, in the heart of human weakness, we are met by the power of God, of the One who is "I AM."

The Bible shows us God who unceasingly seeks each and every one of us: "Where are you?" Let us allow ourselves to be sought by Him, as Saint John of the Cross says: "If the soul seeks God, her God seeks the soul with even more love, infinitely more love." Meeting God's gaze searching for ours, that in itself is already prayer: a gift from the Lord who loved us first.

This union fulfills God's most cherished desires. Why? Using informal vocabulary, Father Marie-Eugène expresses something of God's Mystery: *His very being, His life, is to give Himself; He doesn't know how to do otherwise than to pour out His love, endlessly! We ask: Why am I on earth? There is no need to go looking for little reasons, no, there is only one: God loves us. God has called us out of love; and this love with which God created us is still alive and active. What He has loved, He will always love. What He has given us, He will never take away. What He has begun in you, He will bring to fulfillment* (PP 27).

But isn't this a vain promise; is it still valid for someone who is too far away from God? God is love, without "ifs," without "buts," without exception. "In Him there is only 'yes'," says Paul (2 Cor 1:19). The path of prayer is God and it is Jesus.

Jesus: God who saves, God with us. Jesus: peace walking in the midst of suffering, forgiveness walking in the midst of injustice, the innocent one dying next to the thief. The path of prayer is Him, and it is also us, it's our story where He wants to walk and love: "You are priceless in my eyes, and I love you."

Prayer is there, in this movement full of trust, in this intimate contact in which Our Lord gives Himself deeply. We are seeking this instant. We are not after some kind of innovation; we are moving toward an encounter with Life, with Truth, and with Love. We bring all we are to this encounter; ourselves, without hiding or refusing anything, surrendering ourselves to the One who has always known us: *Jesus is calling us, already, each one of us, by our name that has existed from all eternity; one day we will know it; … that name does exist!* (UD, August 23rd, 1961).

Here I am before you, Lord;
May this moment be entirely Yours.

Prayer is revealed to us as God's gift to the human person; it is up to each one of us to welcome it, for it is also the human person's gift to God.

Made in God's image and likeness, we bear within us a call to reciprocity; our being was created to answer freely in a true exchange. Why does this human response give so much joy to God? Because it is freely given, welling up within and springing forth from a person. Now, when we are free to make this gift, we experience the temptation to flee from it; created for light, we are afraid of light. From within the dissatisfaction and the suffering of this ambiguity, let's allow prayer to well up: let's not wait to be saints in order to pray; let's not wait to be worthy of God in order to draw near Him or to call on Him for help; let's not wait until we know how to pray in order to pray.

How great, then, will be God's joy when He finds a soul that leaves Him entirely free, and in whom He can pour out His love as much as He wants to! *Yes, just as the sun is ready and waiting to enter the house as soon as you open the window, so is God for you.*

Little does it matter where we are on
   the journey.
Humbly, let us give Him this joy.
A wellspring is gushing forth for us:

We need to know our God.
We need to open our hearts
and believe in the incredible love
that is in God,
believe in this immense joy that God finds
in going beyond all the weights and measures
   of justice,
beyond all the barriers of our insufficient merits,
He wants to give freely,
He needs to give freely (CR 26).

SECOND DAY

A MYSTERIOUS LIKENESS

Jesus tells us (cf. Jn 14 and 16):

"Look to your Father, approach Him, live in His Light. Why? Because your Father loves you. The Father's love envelops you. He is lovingly watching over us every single moment – almighty Father, wellspring of Light and Mercy. I am going to the Father. I came from Him; I am going back to Him. Follow me, or rather, do not leave my side: you have lived with me, come with me to the Father."

Our Lord gave testimony to His love for the Father, to the Father's love for Him. He tells us: I assure you that He loves you.

What a source of consolation and joy! We are never isolated, never alone. We have experienced this, but we especially have Our Lord's word: He loves you.... The Holy Spirit from within our souls prays: Abba, Father! He is the Spirit of Sonship, the filial Spirit that takes us back up to the Father. The Spirit dwells in our souls in order to have us enter the intimacy of the Trinity. Jesus, through the life He *pours forth, wants to identify us to Himself, wants to have us enter the Trinity. He is there as the Son, and we enter there as adopted sons and daughters, through our grace.*

The Trinity is our family. We already belong there through faith. Light and darkness! "We will manifest ourselves": this is the fulfillment of Our Lord's irrevocable promise, the fulfillment of the life of our baptismal grace (UD May 1, 1966; June 13, 1965).

The simplicity, the fullness of these texts expressing the unity of the Christian mystery in a single stroke, evokes a mysterious family relationship, a very deep intimacy between God and the human person. Can everyone nourish themselves from this abundant source of life so simply? How can a human being meet God? What can be known about Him, the Unknowable One? The answer is found in this word: grace, something as mysterious as God, "free gift."

Having given human beings life, God did not abandon them to their existence. He had created them from His Father's heart; He stayed with them and drew them to Himself. How? In His Only Son, He granted them participation in His own life: grace; as Father, He made them able to be His children. Each and every one of us can meet God because God has given Himself to us. Through grace, we can love, act, meet Him and discover Him, like children who, by letting themselves be loved, discover their father's love, their mother's love: we are members of God's family. What a marvel! This is the ineradicable source of Father Marie-Eugène's optimism.

But is the door still open for the person whose life has been marked by wrong choices? Yes, God never changes; He has not stopped loving the sinner. How marvelous is His faithfulness! The parable of the prodigal son reveals this paternal trait: he runs to meet his lost child who is coming home; he hugs him tenderly, clothes him with his tunic and gives him the covenant ring. In his extreme love, he makes no reproach, he goes further than forgiveness, he restores his dignity as a son. And he wants joy to resound throughout the whole house!

And what about those who so often live ignoring God, in a world that gets by very well without Him? And what about so many people who will never be baptized? Father Marie-Eugène, who welcomed God's powerful grace into his life and saw it at work all over the world, testifies to this: the all-knowing and all-loving God preceded us and loved us first: you and me, everyone. How? That is the mystery of souls, the mystery of God who keeps hidden in His mercy the secret of the open-hearted person who has not really had access to the Gospel. The Church, the Body of Christ, is more widespread than one might think. But Christ sends us: Go, teach, baptize. Tirelessly did Marie-Eugène strive to reveal to everyone the marvels of baptism which makes us children of God: a treasure ignored by many, even though they have received it.

Baptism (the word means "bath") plunges us into the life of Jesus-Savior, the life that at Easter gushed forth from His side. His side is still open; He brings us to rebirth in His forgiveness. "You have put on Christ," Saint Paul tells us. Can I really dare to believe that He wants to be a part of my own journey? His grace can turn the most hidden existence into eternal splendor. The human person has become "capable of God". The dynamics of the spiritual life, the promise of holiness is there, in this silent seed. And in fact, baptismal water was poured, nothing extraordinary was heard or seen, but at that moment a human being became God's child. A treasure is received and nothing is felt! *Grace seems to sleep within us, beneath a veil of darkness*, like God hidden at Bethlehem. *But being in darkness does not mean God has abandoned us.*

The love of the Three Persons is watching over us: the Father's love, the Son's love, the ever-present and luminous love of the Holy Spirit (UD May 23, 1965). What God shares with us is Himself, His intimate secret: His life. Grace bonds us to each one of the three divine Persons, leads us into the dialogue of their Trinitarian love. Jesus tells us: the Father loves you. Welcoming this word means discovering an invisible and loving Father who bears my life and my eternity. Welcoming this word means finding myself with the Son, in Him: Follow me, He says; *Come with me, I am going to the Father.* Lord, let us walk together. Baptism makes me enter the secret which belongs to Jesus alone: being God's child changes everything! I can say: "Father" as Jesus did, and with Him: "Our Father." The Father has given Him to me as brother and Savior. In Him, I receive this word: You are my beloved Son; in you I place all my love. Too beautiful for me? Within me, in my most intimate center, the Spirit of the Father and the Son breathes His love, which makes me cry out: Abba, Father. There you have it: prayer. The Father is drawing me to Himself, the Son is leading me on, the Spirit is praying within me; my God is here, at work, and I am going to Him.

Prayer is this simple movement of my being, God's child marked by grace. Prayer is the meeting of two loves: God's love for me and my love for God. The Christian never prays alone. I enter Jesus' prayer to His Father, and I can give my prayer to Jesus: I pray with Him and the Holy Spirit sustains my prayer.

> I need only close my eyes, He is there.
> I place all my burdens at His feet.
> May all anxiety be pacified:
> God loves me, Jesus gives me His grace.
> Whether I be trusting, silent
> or in the depths of distress,
> the Spirit joins with me: Abba, Father.
> This cry expresses my desires, my needs,
> my offering.
> I let Him pray within me.
> I follow the movement of my grace
> that turns me toward the Father.
> I thank Him.

Once we are aware of our baptismal grace, the seal it confers, the light it gives, the hopes it bestows, we have an anchor in life. God loves me, God calls me. Of course my sensory nature may shudder, my intellect may be troubled, but I possess the great hope: God Himself (WSB 46).

But where is He?

THIRD DAY

WHERE IS HE?

Silent prayer has us seek God in the center of our soul. Where could we find Him more intimately than in our inner depths where He communicates His divine life, making each one of us personally His child?

God, who is present and acting within me, is truly my Father, for He begets me unceasingly by the outpouring of His life; I can embrace Him myself with a filial embrace in these regions where He is giving Himself. My Lord and my God truly dwells within me; and when my soul is purified enough to receive the power to see God as He is, I will discover Him penetrating, enveloping my soul in those intimate regions where I now seek Him in faith.

All of Heaven lives within my soul. By keeping me in the company of the Holy Trinity who dwells there, silent prayer is more than a preparation for eternal life; it is a real beginning of that very life beneath the veil of faith (JVVD 192).

Where is God? Many are sure of the answer without being able to explain it: "He is with me, within me." Being thus intimately rooted in God is the secret of their peace, whatever happens. *He is here, within me, nowhere more than within me* (UD August 23, 1961). That denotes a powerful experience which happens nowhere else so much as during prayer.

Where is God? Everywhere, of course. God is spirit, and His presence does not imply a physical location. Presence implies relationship. Where is God? He, the One who is, conveys being to His creation. What is God doing right now? He is maintaining in existence the ground I walk on, the air I breathe without thinking about it, the splendor of each sunrise… everything that exists. At every moment this continuous act of creation is happening within each being; this is the active presence of immensity. "The heavens and the earth proclaim His glory," says Psalm 19.

Human beings are also held in existence by this ongoing, silent action. What would I be right now if God was not thinking of me? Not even a trace of dust. Nothing! But no, He is faithful.

"Lord, you know me;
   with all my ways you are familiar.

You knit me in my mother's womb…"
the Psalmist sings (Ps 139).

His wonderful presence does not depend
on our seeking,
He is here, within me, now.

"The heavens and the earth proclaim His glory" but they do not know they are doing so. Now, God created us much greater than a tree or an animal: He made us in His image and likeness. He wants us to participate in His divine nature. With our intelligence, our freedom, and the gift of grace, we can welcome Him, we can call to Him, we can love Him in kind with the very love He gives us. God is present to us in a totally different way: a presence of friendship, an absolutely personal presence. He gives Himself entirely in His self-giving.

Where is God? Within me. At the well-spring of my being; in that deepest of places wherein He begets me; in that deepest of places that can never be violated, never be destroyed; the virginal meeting place, the secret place from whence the Father calls me, where I can trust, where I can answer in complete freedom: in my soul. Unfathomable reciprocity! My God dwells within me.

On this topic, Father Marie-Eugène always quotes Teresa of Avila: The soul is like a castle. In its center lives the King: God. There, very secret things take place between God and the soul. Her dazzling experience of so loving and intimate a Presence within her converted her completely and made her a light for the Church of all times: "I have now begun a new life," she wrote, "God's life within me" (L cf. 200-201).

> A friendly presence: I am never alone,
> however quietly I speak to Him, God hears.
> He is thirsty for my love.
> He gradually increases my ability to receive
>   His gift.
> He always wants to give me more.

God is within me.... I am the one who is so often absent. For many, this is a dramatic situation: in the midst of the incredible mushrooming of discoveries that continually revolutionize all our perspectives, they forget their meaning. "My life: frolicking between two bottomless chasms!" jokes a comic book for young people. Finding God in the center of one's soul and life means finding oneself. It is finding meaning in Him. It is also finding the meaning of earthly things, for the world is not profane. We are the ones who sometimes profane this world, come forth from the Father's hands.

> Lord, I would not exist
> had You not come to me,
> had You not brought me to birth and
>   rebirth in Jesus.
> Lord, I would not know how to meet You
> had You not come to meet me.
> So often have I forgotten You.
> You waited for the right time,
> You waited for me to be ready;
> I disperse myself, curious to know anything
>   about everything;
> From my wandering, call me back.
>   May I find You!
> Give me back to myself,
> by the strength of Your presence.

Prayer is there, so near at hand! How can I enter within myself? "The door of entry to this castle is prayer" (IC I:1), says Teresa of Avila. Something probably has to give: turn off the TV… make a step in His direction.… *God's door is always open to us, and we can enter into Him through prayer. Prayer is contact with a Living God, who reacts with a thrill of joy, with the gift of Himself* (WSB 72-73; 67). To his sister, Father Marie-Eugène wrote: *Go often to seek strength at His side, even when you have nothing to say to Him or you are bored. He will give you an ample reward. He will share Himself with you* (UD November 11, 1921).

"He is alive, the Lord in whose presence I stand!" During his novitiate, the recently ordained Father Marie-Eugène discovered in this Carmelite motto the fundamental axis of his vocation. He wrote to a friend: *Silent prayer is somehow the sun and the center of all the day's activities. Each night one has the impression that this is virtually the only important thing we have done.* This is because in God our human tasks, so necessary in and of themselves, take on an eternal value: *During silent prayer, everything and everyone is present in Jesus, and we can be much more useful to them* (PM 47). Silent prayer is essential because it plunges the soul deeply into God. Christ is your dwelling place. Don't leave Him outside of your life. *Fill your soul with strength and light by a simple contact with God. Surrender yourself to Him, and entrust everything to the Holy Spirit* (PM 142).

Prayer is a friendly exchange,
prayer with no ulterior motives
when we pray for the Good Lord Himself,
without asking for anything, only Him.
Resting in Him,
Loving Him for Himself, loving Him, Himself
                (UD September 5, 1965).
Peacefully keeping watch in faith in
   His presence.
My God, You are here, I am here,
   for Your joy.

Very early on, Father Marie-Eugène encountered a number of lay people inhabited by a deep desire to live in God's presence. He gave them silent prayer which surrenders us to God, rendering us open to His will, for holiness. A young priest gives this testimony: "In my opinion, suggesting a lengthy time of daily silent prayer to priests, to lay people committed to family, professional and social responsibilities, was a prophetic gesture. He needed great audacity, a lot of faith together with a genuine experience to dare to think such a demand could be lived out. Experience demonstrates the fruits of light and faithfulness, balance and inner unity produced by this time given over to prayer."

FOURTH DAY

PRAYING WITH MY WHOLE BEING

Prayer is making contact with God; it is that contact sustained by love. How am I going to make contact with God? By everything I do.

There are three levels of activity in me, three lives: a physical life, an intellectual life, a spiritual, supernatural life. By what means am I going to journey toward God? This will happen using the three levels of activity I possess; I am not going to keep anything back, my whole being will participate.

I have a physical life. I am going to have my body contribute to my search for God: a posture expressing a prayerful attitude before God. In doing that, my body is praying and my soul is already praying too; it is being drawn toward God.

I also have an intellectual life. I think about God. I think of a specific Gospel scene, I make my mental faculties (intelligence, imagination) work. The only reason my will keeps them working is because it loves, it wants to seek God.

We have a third life, the life of grace. This supernatural life is not independent from natural life. It is a life, a participation in God's life; it is the capacity to love God as He loves Himself.

The art of prayer is the synthesis of these three levels of activity, these three lives. Each one needs to have its role, the place and the importance that it rightly has, in order to reach God effectively and efficaciously. I go toward God with my whole being, my three lives actively involved in seeking God.

The big difficulty we experience in silent prayer is the impression that God is not giving Himself. We have an impression of solitude. We cannot perceive the fruit of what God is doing.

Most of the time discouragement comes from the fact that we think we are alone, we trust our impressions.... We need to renew our faith in this truth: the fruit of silent prayer is the fruit of two activities: ours and God's (UD August 19, 1956).

Every human person wants to pray, to meet God. And prayer is indeed this loving meeting between the human person and God. The person praying, however, does encounter difficulties. "I don't know how to pray...." Who among us has not acknowledged this at one time or another?

Father Marie-Eugène demonstrates how prayer is an act which involves the whole person. Our entire being focuses on God in order to meet Him.

"When you pray, go into your inner room and close the door..." (Mt 6:6). What does that mean? Prayer requires a favorable time and place. Now, it is true we are very busy, solicited from all sides.

First of all, we need to know how to find time for prayer: *The Good Lord has the right to have a little time in our lives! He needs us to pay attention to Him, to become more and more aware of supernatural realities ... to become aware of His presence. We have pressing business? The most pressing business is this: finding time for God!* (UD August 2, 1961). Not an instant from time to time, but time wasted for God alone, regularly. And in order to pray, we also need a place that facilitates recollection: the Real Presence of Jesus in the Eucharist, a restful landscape, a pacifying picture.... "Close the door..." close it to noise, to agitation, to preoccupations. Yes! We must want to find the time, a placc; we must understand how necessary this is.

"Pray to your Father who is there in that secret place." God is my Father, I come to Him, trusting, with the certainty that He is here, waiting for me. But I must come; I must take a step.

During prayer, body posture is important. My sensory life participates in my prayer. The Gospel shows us the leper (Lk 17:16), the blind man (Jn 9:38), once healed by Jesus, prostrating themselves before Him. These are examples of prayer that visibly express gratitude through body posture.

A person praying is often depicted with arms outstretched, lifted in praise, or else kneeling in adoration. Body posture, by which the senses are drawn away from the outside world, facilitates recollection and helps the soul to focus on God.

"Pray to your Father who is hidden in that secret place." I am invited to a meeting in the intimacy of my heart. In this same passage (Mt 6), Jesus teaches vocal prayer. But beforehand (Mt 6:7), He warns: "In praying, don't babble on like the Gentiles.... This is how you are to pray: Our Father...." Vocal prayer, spoken or sung, retains its value, provided it is also this aspiration, this gaze toward God.

My thoughts turn toward Him. My prayer may be a meditation on the Word of God: silent reading accompanied by the imagination at work, some reflection; I represent this or that

Gospel scene to myself; I reflect on something Jesus said. This meditation, the work of my natural faculties, in and of itself is not prayer, no more than is body posture, in and of itself. It focuses me on God's presence and only becomes a true meeting, a communion with God when it does not remain solely an intellectual exercise.

I have a third level of life, given to me by God: baptismal grace, divine life, participation in God's very life, which is grafted onto my humanity and makes me capable of entering into an intimate relationship with God.

The art of prayer is a synthesis of these three inseparable lives: physical, intellectual, supernatural. *I go to meet God with my whole being, with all three levels of my life* (UD August 19, 1956). Each one has its role, its place in the unity of my person, but the living and intimate contact with God can only happen through the third level. In order to bring this supernatural love into play, I will use all the resources of my human nature, and, using my free will, I will focus my love on God Himself.

Father Marie-Eugène reminds us how Thérèse of Lisieux, still a child, used to pray silently while looking at pictures. "I would lose the notion of time looking at them," she said (Ms A 31v). These pictures touched her emotionally, and said "so many things" to her that she "was submersed..." in them, that she was totally recollected, as if she had been *plunged* into God, united to Him.

It is up to each one of us to find *what works*, what recollects us, to vary our methods; *when a method is worn out, find another one.* Any means: body posture and gestures, spiritual reading, meditation, are good as long as they are like springboards allowing our filial love to spring up.

Silent prayer is personal: depending on the moment, our age, our temperament, *we will have a practically infinite variety of contacts with God. This should keep us away from systematizing* (UD August 19, 1956). That tells us something about how free with God the soul can be.

"Your Father who sees what is hidden will reward you" (Mt 6:6). Then God fills us to overflowing with His love: this is the fruit of prayer.

However we *feel* nothing. The temptation to be discouraged may nip at our heels. So we need to know what faith is, how it is used in prayer.

FIFTH DAY

HAVE FAITH IN YOUR FAITH

What is the essential condition in order to touch God, to receive His grace and His mercy? What sort of cooperation does the Good Lord require in order to diffuse this love in our souls? John of the Cross has pinpointed this essential condition: faith.

Our Lord's presence here below allows us to see faith in action and shows us what we need to do in order to make contact with God. Let's look at the centurion's faith in the Gospel (Mt 8:5-13).

"I am not worthy to have you enter under my roof; only say the word and my servant will be healed." What does the centurion demonstrate here? His trust in Our Lord. See this faith in Our Lord's transcendence that goes beyond any tangible means and is all-powerful. See how Our Lord's soul thrills, see the contact this faith makes. "Amen, I say to you, in no one in Israel have I found such faith." Then He said to the centurion: "Go your way; Let it be done for you as you have believed." We get a

glimpse of faith in action. This is not an ephemeral event. It is one of the laws of God's action, a law of the spiritual life.

John of the Cross says: "Faith is the only means to reach God" (AMC, II, 9, 1). Faith truly reaches God. Our intelligence does not reach God; infinity separates it from God. How can this distance be crossed, how can we touch God, God who is Love, God who is Life? By faith.

Faith is an antenna that makes us cross the infinite distance that separates us from God. Faith reaches God with such power that God diffuses Himself, because God is Love, because God is a blazing fire. Place a piece of paper in contact with a blazing fire: it burns (UD April 6, 1966).

Father Marie-Eugène wanted to help those who are beginning to put prayer in their lives and who may be disconcerted by the impression that they aren't reaching God. So he continually taught how important the place and role of faith are in our relationship with God.

Why faith?

By means of our intelligence, we are capable of acknowledging that there is a God (Rom 1:20), but there it is a matter of simple natural knowledge that cannot unite us to God. For God is not an idea that I can grasp by reasoning, in the same way He is not a thing that I can touch with my hand; God is Someone.

Someone who came to meet us: He spoke to us by His Son Jesus. "No one has ever seen God. The only Son, God who is nearest to the Father's heart, has made Him known" (Jn 1:18). God, through His Son, came to reveal to us the depths of His mystery of love. He came to tell us who He is, and that we are called to be His children. To be one with Him, He has given us His life, grace which has its own means of action: faith, hope and charity.

What is supernatural faith?

"Faith is the theological virtue by which we believe in God..." (*Catechism of the Catholic Church*, #1814), in the Word of God deposited in the Scriptures and entrusted to the Church. *Theological* means that this virtue is capable of reaching God Himself, as He revealed Himself in Jesus Christ. It is a gift from God received at Baptism. Faith alone establishes a personal relationship with God; faith alone can penetrate God's mystery because faith alone is adapted to knowing this mystery: "God, alone... dwelling in unapproachable light. No one has ever seen or can ever see Him" (I Tim 6:16). Faith alone allows us to reach Him.

Let's look at Jesus talking to Nicodemus (Jn 3:1–21). He doesn't answer his questions the way a teacher explaining God's mystery would. No, He invites this reasonable man who is relying on his intelligence, to enter the mystery. "We speak of what we know and we bear witness to what we have seen.... For God so loved the world that He gave His only Son so that anyone who believes in Him may have eternal life." Jesus is the witness; He comes from God.

Nicodemus is invited to base his faith on the Word of God. He understands that our intelligence cannot envelop, grasp by itself the Infinite One, God. It can only adhere to the mystery; it cannot reach God on its own.

"Who do you say that I am?" Jesus asks His apostles. "You are the Messiah, the Son of the living God!" (Mt 16:15–17). Here Peter's faith reaches the very mystery of the person of Christ. This confession of faith does not come from "flesh and blood", human ways of knowing, but has been revealed by the Father.

An act of faith is a positive step, an act accomplished by the virtue of faith. This virtue of faith is grafted onto the intelligence, like a graft on the vine stock. How often did Father Marie-Eugène develop this comparison! Many at Notre-Dame de Vie still remember the walks on the plateau overlooking the shrine: we were off to see the vine stock being grafted.

What does the vine dresser do when he grafts the vine stock? He takes a slip of the variety of grape he wants, he attaches it to the vine stock destined to provide sap; the vine stock, thanks to its roots, draws from the ground the nourishment the graft needs. Well, our intelligence is like the original vine stock; faith is grafted onto it. The supernatural, divine life within us does not exist in and of itself; it is grafted onto our human faculties. The human person is unified; my three lives are inseparable. The vine graft will produce its own fruit, not that of the original vine stock. In the same way, faith will produce its own act, a supernatural act. So I can reach God because faith is made to do that, to touch the infinite: that is its privilege. An act of faith allows the whole human person to be in communion with God. There is no difference in nature between seeing God in Heaven and faith on earth.

When I die, my eyes will be open; I will not see anything other than what I see now in faith, Father Marie-Eugène used to say.

But it is not enough to have a good graft. You need to nourish the trunk and the roots of the vine stock so it can carry the sap to nourish the graft that will bear fruit.

Difficulties with prayer may come from the fact that the vine stock is not getting enough nourishment. We need to take up the Sacred Scriptures, read them and meditate on them within the faith of the Church. We need to receive the life of Christ through the sacraments administered by the Church. But God can only be *touched* by an act of faith.

God is Love; Love is essentially a self-diffusing power. Marie-Eugène explained this in his down-to-earth language:

> *God is a flaming blaze, a fire, a fountain, an ocean. When I make contact with God through faith, we can compare that to fire: I place my hand in fire, it burns me; I place it in water, it gets wet. What I receive when I touch God through faith is divine life. The living God, the life of God inundates me* (UD August 19, 1956).
>
> Let's have faith in our faith!

Whatever our impressions may be, God is here.

Let's not risk hearing Jesus' reproach to His apostles: "Where is your faith?" (Lk 8:25).

God, any time, day or night, I can be united to You.

I believe, and I remain peaceful in Your presence.

SIXTH DAY

SAFE IN DARKNESS

Faith is not obvious truth; faith is obscure knowledge.

It seems that our act of faith finds nothing but darkness. Yes! That is usually what we experience. Through the darkness, however, we do touch God. Faith reaches God. The Gospel affirms this to us; some Gospel scenes show us that's the way it is. We need to believe this Gospel law; we need to believe we are enlightened by faith. The Good Lord makes us feel obscurity; He only wants to blind our intelligence; that is the normal effect of God's light.

We could readily say that faith is almost an act of love. It's a commitment.

The Gospel shows us the sinful woman who goes to Simon the Pharisee's house and anoints Jesus' feet with costly perfume (Lk 7:36-50): "Your faith has saved you, go in peace!" The sinful woman manifests her love. And Our Lord praises her for her faith: faith which is an act of love, which is a surrender of self. It is a gift of the person, a commitment of the person. This woman was moved by sorrow for her sins; her whole being went to find Our Lord and show her submission. When she leaves, she has been transformed. I'm quoting the Gospel; I'm not making it up. These are things we would hardly dare to say were they not found in the Gospel.

The irreplaceable role of faith in the spiritual life needs to be stressed. It is a reasonable adherence; it is a commitment. If there is no self-giving, commitment as the sinful woman showed, faith is not complete. But when self-giving is there, the Good Lord gives Himself and there is union between God and me. This faith is obscure and consequently its effects are not perceived by either the intelligence or the senses.

The initial act of adherence is hard; once the commitment is made, the Good Lord gives His love which gradually effects a transformation. Faith is in the commitment. We need to cross through the darkness, through the fog; we need to make the commitment. Whatever the obstacles that stand between God and us may be, through faith we can overturn the obstacles and establish contact with God (UD April 6, 1966).

I pray. I touch God by faith, yes!... But I cannot feel anything, I find nothing but darkness. Do I have faith? We need to understand that "faith is a night" and that I cannot depend on what I feel.

Night: for whom? And why? Essentially for my sensitivity and my intelligence that are not adapted to the supernatural. My senses are adapted to the tangible world and my intelligence is made for the clarity of ideas. While the act of faith does require the intelligence, nonetheless the intelligence remains blinded by transcendence, by God's Infinity. Our God is "a hidden God" (Is 45:15), a hidden God who reveals Himself; a revealed God who remains the hidden God.

John of the Cross keeps on repeating that "faith is a dark night for souls" but he immediately adds: "in this way it gives them light ... by blinding them on the natural level, it illumines them.... Faith lies beyond our understanding, taste, feeling and imaginings" (AMC II 3:4; 4:2), and that is why it is knowledge in darkness.

Faith buries the intelligence in God's mystery. It does not at all destroy the intellectual human knowledge that serves as a basis to the act of faith, but it goes further, beyond ideas, toward God alone, to *plunge* into Him. The intelligence adheres to God's truth, even though it does not grasp it clearly. But believing is not only adhering intellectually, it is also making a personal commitment. Faith, a gift from God, also depends on an act of free will. During silent prayer, I am not trying to understand God; I am trying to meet Him, to unite myself to Him with my whole being, to enter into His mystery through the contact of living faith.

Faith is a life. And it is love – supernatural charity – that guides the soul in the night of faith. The forgiven sinful woman manifested her faith by demonstrating a great deal of love (Lk 7:47); hers was a gesture of love.

"Faith and love are the two leaders of the blind who will take you by paths unknown to you, as far as the secret chasms of God," John of the Cross says once again (*Spiritual Canticle*, B stanza 1, 11).

Father Marie-Eugène would often show how our Blessed Mother is a model of faith. Mary lived at her Son's side in the darkness of divine mystery. With absolute certainty, she knew she had borne the Savior within her. Her Annunciation fiat was a commitment in faith as well as a loving response; and she lived on faith. "Blessed is she who believed!" (Lk 1:45). Using Elizabeth's words, what the Holy Spirit exalts is Mary's faith. Faith: certainty and at the same time, darkness! *No one has experienced darkness more profoundly than our Blessed Mother because no one has entered so deeply into God's mystery* (P 178).

To the woman who cried out from amidst the crowd: "Blessed is the woman who bore you," Jesus answered: "Rather, blessed are those who hear the Word of God and keep it" (Lk 11:27–28). Bearing the Savior in her womb is not what made Mary "blessed." What Jesus praised His Mother for was her faith; Mary is "blessed" because she believed God's word. And to the apostle Thomas, "the Doubter," who professed his faith after touching the body of the Risen One – "My Lord and my God!" – Jesus revealed the beatitude of faith: "Blessed are those who have not seen and have believed" (Jn 20:29).

> Oh God, in this darkness where I am,
> I believe that You are here.
> I cannot see but I believe.
> I believe that You are at my side.
> Guide me toward the far off glimmer of
> light that attracts me despite the darkness

that envelops me.
And it is in the very heart of darkness
that faith is a source of light.
"With no other light or guide
than the one that burned in my heart.
O guiding night!
O night more lovely than the dawn!"

(DN stanzas 3; 5)

In this life of faith, there is an experience
which holds no glimmer for the intelligence,
but which is certainty for the soul:
God is present, alive!
God Light… God Love…
We remain in darkness,
but the soul is as if *held* by this darkness.
God gives Himself, God holds us.

Light springs forth not from the intelligence but from love. In this darkness, the exchange that happens between God and the soul is not an exchange of ideas; it is an exchange of love. That is a source of light of another kind, indeed! It is a knowledge that comes from love, an adherence that is a movement of love. Faith is in the firmness of the adherence which engages the person: a living faith, a loving faith, a faith that blossoms in hope and leads to the soul's union with God.

> *In this darkness, the soul journeys safely.*
> *Is not the Master awake within!*
> *The soul is no longer alone…*
> *Dimly aware of this … she is happier than*
>   *she has ever been;*
> *She is walking safely in the light*
> *of the living flame that is burning in her heart*
>   (JVVD 559).

SEVENTH DAY

THE HOLY SPIRIT, OUR FRIEND, IS HERE

Let us make an act of faith in this Holy Spirit who is in our souls. The Holy Spirit is not a thought; He is Someone who is the Life of our soul, the living Breath, the Guest of our soul constantly acting in us unceasingly. He is an intelligent and loving Person who dwells in us.

We should therefore resolve to live with the Holy Spirit, and seek Him out frequently.

When we enter within ourselves to examine our conscience and attitudes, the first thing we ought to seek, indeed almost the only thing, is the Holy Spirit dwelling within us. He is there as our friend, our Guest. He, the architect of the Church, the worker of our sanctification, is there. He who builds the Church, the great work in which He associates us, is there.

We do not ask this Holy Spirit to reveal His presence to us by another Pentecost, or by striking outward manifestations, but to deign to reveal His presence to us at least by giving us faith in Him.

As Our Lord says, rivers of living water will flow out from the heart of the one who believes in Him; the Holy Spirit pours Himself out through this soul. Floods of life and light rush upon souls through the Holy Spirit, but they pass particularly through this soul who has opened the divine flood gates by faith (WSB 215–216).

Jesus said: "I will send you the Holy Spirit from the Father" (Jn 15:26). The Holy Spirit prolongs and completes the mission of Jesus Christ. Inseparable from the Father and the Son, the Holy Spirit dwells personally within me, I am His beloved dwelling place: "God's love has been poured out into our hearts through the Holy Spirit who has been given to us" (Rom 5:5). He responds to love; within me He prays the Son's cry: "Abba."

When I pray, I make acts of faith and love that put me in communion with God. In and of itself, faith is perfect; it "gives" God according to John of the Cross. But often I am restless… everything comes back to me: my imaginary world, my doubts, what has upset me, what worries me…. God seems to me to be elsewhere. "Silent prayer is a conversation," but how can I make it last when I do not get anything out of it? What is human is not adapted to the invisible God. I need to be pacified within in order to remain near Jesus and receive His grace. After silent prayer I am full of good intentions. Then, at the first opportunity, I fall. I need inner support in order to carry out a specific action beyond my strength that God is asking of me, to persevere in my vocation, to accomplish my mission.

> "Lord, I believe in You, I love You.…"
> These are truly my words,
> and You hear them.
> But, more than words,
> You want my heart and all that I am.
> Left to myself, how can I pray
> otherwise than with my poor words?
> Who will carry me to You?

"The Holy Spirit comes to the aid of our weakness" (Rom 8:26). By His gifts He supports my faculties to help them in their activity. I go to God through God, and with my whole being.

Just as the sail allows the ship to move forward by the wind's direct action, the gifts allow me to be receptive to the breath of the Holy Spirit. In the darkness of prayer, this Breath pacifies me, gives me strength and light. Thanks to Him, my faith can peacefully maintain its contact with God. Thanks to Him, once again, the indication I need in order to act in a specific unsolvable family or professional situation becomes visible. At certain crossroads of my life, He is the one who guides and bolsters my liberty so as to be able to answer God's call and remain faithful to Him. Step by step, God's hand holds mine. *God's interventions through the gifts of the Holy Spirit may become so frequent and so profound that they establish the soul in a state of practically constant dependence upon Him* (JVVD 307).

Our experience of God is astonishing: I may be in the dark and receive abundant light, feel my weakness and go straight to what God is asking of me. I may be anxious and at the same time know a peace and joy that cannot be felt. I can still hear Father Marie-Eugène saying: It's useless to try and stop the distractions; to regain peace, go beyond them, escape into God! Do not abandon silent prayer, the contact of faith; hold on to Him as best you can in the darkness, because that is where He is. Even if you cannot calm down, God has given Himself. After prayer, do you want to go back to it? See, you do indeed get something out of it! So… flounder about! God's action is real and deep even if it is paradoxical. *Whether He be a calm ocean or come as a tempest, you will take Him as He wants to give Himself…* (UD May 16, 1959). But I fall! If you fall, if you no longer know what you are about, pray; call the Holy Spirit, give Him your difficulties, give yourself to Him. Do not expect your prayer to have an immediate result. Wait for the slow diffusion of charity that will raise you up. Yes, He wants to save your whole being and to do that, He is giving Himself to you.

> *Union with the Holy Spirit is not a luxury, no. In our daily work, human techniques have their importance, but the first thing to do is to bond ourselves with the One who is at work. This bond is built by an act of faith, but only repeated acts will truly fashion intimacy, friendship with Him. In order to work, we need to be with Him always, to have a sort of reflex to check in with Him each time we want to do something.*
>
> *May He always be here, and may we always be with Him* (UD August 1, 1960).

Gradually, with my whole being, I am going to live a new life in this Spirit who adapts me to

Himself: detachment and joy, balance and flexibility. He uses them! The Acts of the Apostles shows the Apostles' transformation at Pentecost: strength, light, even eloquence! "You too will testify" (Jn 15:27).

The Holy Spirit makes the martyrs' witness burst forth, that of the saints who respond to people's needs in such creative and appropriate ways. "The Spirit itself bears witness with our spirit" (Rom 8:16) for a profound conversion, for healing, so that God's light may be integrated into our intelligence, our freedom, even our emotional expression, in order to announce a message of hope and recreated humanity. Hidden among the treasures and the weakness of the human person, the Spirit unveils the inheritance of Christ.

He is alive, the Spirit of love who dwells within me and who seized me so long ago. My holiness will be to believe in His presence, to surrender to His grasp....

Such intimate sharing, so unusual for Father Marie-Eugène, lets us suppose that with the Holy Spirit we touch, so it would seem, the mystery of his grace. My whole life, as he also said, *has been based on knowing, discovering the Holy Spirit.*

Like a father, he expressed his wish. Let us place ourselves in his prayer:

> *May the Holy Spirit descend upon you;*
> *as soon as possible, may you be able to say that*
> *the Holy Spirit is your friend,*
> *the Holy Spirit is your light,*
> *the Holy Spirit is your Master.*
> *This is how I pray for you and*
> *– know this well – it is the prayer*
> *that I am going to continue praying*
> *and that I will continue praying for you throughout*
> *eternity* (UD February 21, 1965).

EIGHTH DAY

THE PRICE OF FREEDOM

The spiritual life is founded on the collaboration between two activities: ours and God's. But God respects our freedom. He will never sanctify us without our free will. He has created us free so that we can live out the complete gift of ourselves. He wants our cooperation in the work He wants to carry out in our souls. Therein lays the mystery of divine activity and ours.

The gift of self! It is not just a passing act. It is not just for today, but for tomorrow and the day after tomorrow and always. May our spiritual life be an ongoing gift of self, repeated and lived out with greater and greater humility.

The perfect act of love is self-giving.

To see the value of this gift of self, we need to look at Our Lord. "When He came into the world, Christ said: Behold, I come to do Your will, O God" (Heb 10:5). The first gesture of Christ's humanity was self-giving. And when He died, there was another act of surrender that would sum up His whole life and echo the first: "Father, into Your hands I commend my spirit" (Lk 23:46). These two gestures of Christ demonstrate how much the gift of ourselves is worth.

We could say that Our Lord's whole "spiritual life" was composed of self-giving, offering Himself up to fulfill God's plan. The day He was with the Samaritan woman on the rim of the well of Shechem and the apostles brought Him something to eat, He told them: "My food is to do the will of the One who sent me" (Jn 4:34). That reveals Christ's soul to us. He loved His Father and He surrendered Himself to His Father.

In our own personal sanctification, in building the Mystical Body of Christ, that is to say, in His whole work of mercy, God wants our human freedom to collaborate with Him. As the foundation of everything, the basis for this collaboration, there needs to be the gift of all that we are.

(UD July 24, 1944;UD August 2, 1961)

"If you knew the gift of God..." Jesus told the Samaritan woman (Jn 4:10). At the beginning, there is God's gift. He has the initiative in giving every gift from creation to the salvation of humanity.

In giving us His Son, the Father revealed His love to us and made the gift of Himself.

Within the love that unites Him to His Father, Jesus lived out the complete gift of Himself. He appeared on earth and He gave His life, freely: "The Father loves me because I lay down my life.... I lay it down on my own" (Jn 10:17–18).

An essential disposition of Christ, the complete gift of self is an essential disposition of every Christian (JVVD 328). Grace, participation in God's life, is filial. It makes us sons and daughters, in the image of Christ, the only Son. We can only be united to God by *being identified with Christ*, by living in His movement of love toward the Father, and by conforming our lives "to the attitude that is in Christ" (Phil 2:5). Our self-giving is the highest expression of our liberty. Its worth can be seen in light of Christ's total gift, His free and obedient love for His Father.

The foundation of the spiritual life is this gift, coming forth from a free person. It is love's response to God's extravagant love for us.

Teresa of Avila warns us: "God does not force our will; He takes what we give Him; but He does not give Himself completely until we give ourselves completely to Him" (WP 28: 12).

This means that the gift answers the gift. To the complete self-giving of God's love the Christian responds by total self-giving to God, receiving thereafter a share in a love that is more and more irresistible and fulfilling, a charity that enlivens more and more. Such are the dynamics of the gift that leads us to live out our Christian vocation perfectly.

To be true, our self-giving needs to have certain qualities. Father Marie-Eugène enumerated these:

It is an *absolute* gift, without any restrictions or preconceived ideas. It is not a "yes, but...." It is saying yes to the Gospel's radical expectations: "If you want to be perfect, go, sell everything..." (Mt 19:21). An absolute gift liberates us! Each day, God calls me. My love's response will be my daily self-giving up to my last breath.

Teresa of Avila also says – is there a tinge of sadness? – "We are so slow in giving ourselves entirely to God... there is no end to our preparations" (L 11:1).

This *absolute* gift is a gift in *darkness*, an *indeterminate* gift. There is a certain danger that we might determine it according to our tastes, our preferences; it is important not to let ourselves get caught in the trap of imagination, and illusion is always a possibility. From this perspective, Marie-Eugène talked about a *spirituality of events: our faith needs to be attentive to providential situations...*

sources of light and grace (JVVD 608). Are not events and situations often the most trustworthy messengers of God's will, since we know, in faith, that God is Providence? For those who love Him, "God works in every way for their good…" (Rom 8:28). He uses events.

How far can we be led by this commitment in *darkness*, this *indeterminate* quality in achievements? Might we be led all the way to Gethsemane? Let's not try to find out. The gift is not found in the effort needed to make it; it is in the movement of love that puts us in communion with God. What is essential is living out a more and more generous and disinterested faithfulness in love.

Self-giving *identifies us profoundly with Christ*. It is not some *superficial imitation of Christ …* manifesting *empty external formalism*, but a constant disposition that *surrenders us to Christ's grace within us* (JVVD 328). A permanent "yes" to God's love, the gift of ourselves renewed each day can only attract Love and make us enter into the depths of His fathomless mystery.

For in the Church, each one of us has a mission; our self-giving associates us with God's undertaking. We are the branches that bear fruit inasmuch as they remain on the vine stock (Jn

15:4–5). Thus our own undertakings, however modest they may be, acquire the fruitfulness of divine undertakings.

In this collaboration, God trusts the human person, and that renders our self-giving more and more *humble*. What did the Virgin Mary say when faced with the collaboration the Holy Spirit was asking of her? "He has looked upon His handmaid's lowliness" (Lk 1:48). God asked her for her *fiat*: "May it be done to me according to your word" (Lk 1:38). In this call, Mary saw only her Lord's merciful gaze. She said yes unreservedly: there she was, associated with the mystery of the Incarnation, the Redemption, God-Trinity's highest undertaking. There she was, called to become the Mother of the Church.

"Jesus wills that we have a share with Him in the salvation of souls. He wills to do nothing without us," wrote Thérèse of Lisieux (LT 135). In the Church, there is a multiple variety of missions and vocations because they are personal. But they all are expressions of love, self-giving to God for the Church: "Love alone makes the members of the Church act…. Love comprises all vocations, Love is everything," Thérèse exclaimed (Ms B 3v).

NINTH DAY

IN THE HUMDRUM OF ORDINARY LIFE

Why did Our Lord, who willed to spend thirty-three years on earth, spend thirty of them in solitude? … Why did Jesus do that even though He had such a great mission and so much work to do? He wanted to lead that life to satisfy a need for adoration and prayer, to live an ordinary life. Nazareth shows the perfection of the Incarnation. He was truly a man who experienced our human condition; He lived it just as we do.

He wanted to show us that in order to accomplish our mission, however broad it may be, we need to do so by living our ordinary lives. As for extraordinary things, we will do them when God entrusts them to us. Ordinary things are the fabric of our lives; in doing them we are called to become holy and serve the Church. Thérèse of the Child Jesus had an astonishingly truthful perspective on this (LC August 20, 1897). She said: I do not like made-up stories. She often brought to light the mishaps of daily life, for example: Joseph may not have been paid… there may have been complaints about his work… perhaps there were little incidents like we have with our neighbors… little things that made him suffer.…

God calls us to that. People would seemingly like to do extraordinary things, make use of a marvelous power in order to do good and help everyone. Life in Nazareth was not like that; it was ordinary life with its little incidents, its monotony, almost nothing.… And under that ordinary life, God's intense life was hidden; a life of faith, of love, of hope as well, for this ordinary atmosphere did not keep hope from being alive, and how intensely! Mary and Joseph lived in darkness, but their hope was powerful, alive, yearning for fulfillment. They knew very well that He, Jesus, would do everything

(UD August 20, 1955).

This passage speaks for itself. In making a covenant with each and every one of us, God does not usually change our condition, He transfigures it. Any existence can be taken over, taken up by Him.

A practical question comes up here: how can I sustain contact with God in the midst of multiple calls that upset schedules and plans? Do I need to "choose the better part" and push away the solicitations of life? Or should I welcome them as coming from God? Marie-Eugène made this affirmation: both calls come from Him, just like a car has brakes adapted to the engine's power. Contemplative life itself is also comprised of a large amount of work willed and blessed by God. There needs to be some discernment, not by means of too human an equilibrium, but in faithfulness to our duty of state which manifests God's specific will, and in availability to respond to the Holy Spirit's flame burning within us. God gives His light. *I have worked hard all my life*, Marie-Eugène acknowledged. And when the quantity of work was overwhelming, he would pray even longer, drawing light and strength there.

For him, prayer and action could never work against each other; he understood the spiritual life globally: these two parts participate in the same movement of self-giving to the Holy Spirit. In the active life, love that comes from prayer is the most necessary factor so that the Christian may participate in God's ongoing work of creation, animating it with His Spirit. The power of faith has visible effects. The time spent with God flows back out in love for Him and our brothers and sisters. That is why Father Marie-Eugène also suggested that we go back to God during the day, connecting with Him by little "plunges" into Him, short and deep, no less important than silent prayer. *As soon as we have a free moment, God needs to be there* (UD January 29, 1960).

The mystery of Jesus can enlighten us about ordinary life. God became man; His great victories were carried out discreetly and even in apparent failure: the manger, the cross. God seemed to be asleep... annihilated. There you have it! The weak child of Bethlehem, who came from the depths of God and touched the earth with so much love, recreated humanity without making any noise. We always think that for good to happen it has to be glamorous. Jesus' life at Nazareth, Mary and Joseph themselves, reveal the most precious realities of our simple lives. Joseph humbly served where he was supposed to be. Humility here means accepting to be what God wants us to be, inside and out. When we thus live the gift of self, God unites us to Himself in the depths of our being; deep within, the action of grace – hidden because divine – mysteriously incorporates us into Christ. How?

Grace is grafted within us as our participation in God's life becoming truly, very deeply and intimately one with each and every one of us, taking on our individual temperaments, the very fibers of our being, our uniqueness, even our wounds. Grace infiltrates, dilates, heals. God is glorified by what He has saved. That is why no part of our lives is indifferent to or absent from Him, everything has its importance and God puts nothing between parentheses. And that is why, if I agree, each moment of my life will receive His visit. Each moment will be this meeting, this treasure, this act of love. That is where He comes to find me. Grace is filial: children constantly draw from their Father's treasure, expecting everything from Him. And when our union with Him is complete, John of the Cross affirms that "all our actions are divine" (LF stanza 1) and useful to the world. Nazareth shows the perfection of the incarnation and its consequences.

Count on your grace, said Father Marie-Eugène. "My grace" is a surprising expression: Christ's singular gift for me, the white stone entrusted to me, the personal mystery of my life and my divine vocation, enlightened in every detail.

If we sometimes take the monotony to be mediocrity, let us not be afraid to give it to Jesus so that He can raise it up to the extent of God's plan. In the darkness, Mary and Joseph are calling us. If their life was ordinary on the outside, there was nothing ordinary about their inner lives. Adoration nourished them, silent love illuminated them. There we can see what God expects of us for the world. Our part is necessary, God's part is sovereign: *They knew everything would be done by Him*. Our part, day by day, is to follow Him and cooperate by believing and loving, by our trusting gaze. Explicit testimony is necessary, but our simple lives, even if we do not see it, radiate hope and announce Jesus.

> Who, more than Joseph,
> lived close to Mary, to Jesus?
> What did he see? Nothing extraordinary.
> The gaze of his faith went beyond the silence to go farther,
> into the depths of the mystery.
> May he be our Master of silent prayer.
> May he teach us
> to read the Gospel in its pure light
> which discloses truth itself to us,
> and the hope that truth bears.
> Close to him, close to Mary,
> may Jesus be enough for us.

TENTH DAY

BIRDS' WINGS

What is hope? A theological virtue.

By faith we touch God: faith is an antenna made to grasp God. Charity unites us to God: when we love God we are transformed into Him.

What is hope in the spiritual life? The virtue that keeps us going. It does for us what wings do for birds. It keeps us moving toward God; it makes us progress in the spiritual life. We move toward God inasmuch as we hope. It is really important to foster the virtue of hope, to fortify its wings.

We need to know what hope is. Often in this area we are the victims of ignorance. Hope is confused with feeling. I am full of fervor so I have hope; but hope is not always expressed fervently.

Hope is a virtue by which we long for God, we wait for God, we know that God will come and will be given to us. And not only God, but the means to reach Him....

To explain "the mechanism" of hope we need to

understand that it can go toward God for whom it longs in two ways:

1. By moving: I am longing for God, so I go to look for Him; the child who wants to hug his mother goes toward her.

2. Someone wants to go toward God and cannot do so. During prayer, for example, my mind finds nothing; my will is powerless; I cannot reach God, so I sigh and I yearn (UD June 9, 1959).

Hope provokes two attitudes: a positive attitude of moving toward God and an attitude of waiting. The second movement, an attitude of patience, is usually the stronger during silent prayer.

(UD February 15, 1966)

The theological virtues are inseparable. We only distinguish them in order to demonstrate the *mechanism* of the spiritual life more clearly. By faith, I *touch* God; faith is the basis of our relationship with God. Hope provides the dynamics of faith prompting us to go deeper and deeper into the depths of God. Charity unites us to God; it is an act of union, the perfect filial act.

What is hope about?

Hope is a theological virtue by which we trustingly await all that God has promised us in His Son Jesus. The certainty of hope is based on the certainty of faith. Hope leads us on into the depths of the mystery of God's love that we know by faith.

"You made us for Yourself, O Lord, and our hearts are restless until they rest in You," said Saint Augustine of Hippo. God Himself imprinted this desire in our hearts. We are waiting for God and from Him alone are we waiting and hoping for what He has promised.

"Father, I desire that they, too, may be with me where I am – those You have given me – so they may see the glory You have given me" (Jn 17:24). Such are Jesus' words; such is our hope, for God is infinitely faithful in His promises.

The apostle Paul explains: "We walk by faith, not by sight" (2 Cor 5:7). "It was through hope we were saved. But a hope that can be seen isn't truly a hope. After all, who hopes for what they can already see? But if we hope for what we do not yet see, then we wait patiently" (Rom 8:24–25).

Hope is a hunger for God, for God whom we cannot see, cannot feel, and whom nonetheless we desire because He loves us. Father Marie-Eugène, using concrete examples as he always did, very simply illustrated hope's twofold movement, the two attitudes it provokes:

Jesus is in the tabernacle in the chapel. I'm going to go there and seek Him. There you have hope. But it doesn't work, I can't find Him, so I'm going to wait.... I know that He too is seeking me.... In order to wait for Him to come, I need to work at it, I need to open up my soul. You see the twofold movement of hope. The first is active; the second is passive: it is patience (UD February 15, 1966).

It is patience, rather than passivity that does nothing. I need to open my soul by a gaze of faith and wait for God who can seem far from us for we are waiting for Him in darkness.

"I wait for the Lord with all my soul,
I hope for the fulfillment of His Word.
My soul waits for the Lord
more eagerly than sentinels for daybreak."

(Ps 130)

The "endurance" Paul talks about is perseverance. That means knowing how to remain steadfast while waiting, in the darkness of faith, or even with distractions; in other words, during dryness in silent prayer.

Praying is believing and hoping. It is waiting for what is not within our power to obtain on our own; waiting for what God alone will give us.

Can we hope for anything else besides God

alone as we pray to Him? For example, can we hope to be healed? There are "temporal" goods that we may ask for, but God often leads us by unsettling pathways that we do not understand. Our prayer needs to become very humble. Cardinal Journet shared this fact: in the chapel of Bourguillon in Switzerland, an ex-voto offering bore this thanksgiving prayer written in gilded letters: "Oh Mary, thank you for not granting my prayer." Theological hope waits only for God, only because of Him and for His joy which is to give Himself.

> My God, I hope in You.
> I cry out to You with my whole being,
> I reach out to You.
> But I know, in the depths of my heart,
> that You are the one who is calling me to You.

John of the Cross, so often quoted by Marie-Eugène, wrote: "The soul must be detached from all that is not God in order to be united to God.… Possession of any kind is indeed opposed to hope, and this virtue, as St. Paul said, has as its object what we do not possess" (AMC III 15).

In the spiritual itinerary, hope – the virtue that keeps us moving – is going to grow and be perfected by freeing itself of anything that is in the way of its journey toward God. This journey will be marked by stages in detachment. The rich young man who asked Jesus: "What must I do to inherit eternal life?" (Lk 18:18), certainly felt the increasing demands of hope within him. What Jesus suggested to him: "Sell all you have and distribute it to the poor..." was only the first stage in his journey toward the "treasure" of eternal life.

"Where your treasure is, there also will your heart be" (Mt 6:21). Where is our treasure? In order for the bird to fly, in order for it to be able to spread its wings, nothing must be holding it back. The lighter its flight, the higher it will go. It is the same with theological hope. There are riches that hinder us from going to God because they are treacherous underpinnings and in some ways we think more of them than we do of God. The true riches toward which hope needs to tend are those which have an eternal value.

If we want to possess God, we need to remember that *God will only fill the space that our detachment leaves free for Him* (UD February 15, 1966). The time for spiritual hope is the time of spiritual poverty, a painful time, but little by little it sets the bird free until nothing more stops its flight toward God.

ELEVENTH DAY

TRUSTING TO THE POINT OF AUDACITY

John of the Cross linked the virtue of hope to spiritual poverty. This hope, whether it be in order to go toward what it desires — God — or in order to yearn for Him, does so all the better the poorer it is. Poverty makes hope strong and perfect. In order to be able to hope, we need to be poor.

Spiritual childhood is based on the doctrine of poverty and hope. It is the keystone of Thérèse of Lisieux's way of childhood, its theological foundation.

How are we to live out this spiritual childhood that is going to ask us to live on hope? This life requires that we realize that we are God's children, that we really believe it, that we act like children do with God. This is what flows from the nature of our grace. With God, what does a child need to do? To be united to Him, to maintain contact with Him.

How can this union with the Good Lord be sustained? By feeling our weakness, by experiencing our weakness. Our filial grace is only awake and continually active thanks to this experience of our weakness. This is the feeling we need to accept and use. The poverty that we experience in our spiritual life, in prayer, instead of turning us in upon ourselves, should launch us toward the Good Lord. There you have the gesture of trust we can make; God is waiting for this act of hope in His mercy.

These are realities, not mere words. Poverty makes hope grow, and it makes us hope in God alone.

Who will be the greatest in the Kingdom of Heaven? The one who is the littlest (see Mk 10:15), who has nothing, but who makes the gesture of the child who turns toward God, waiting for everything from God. The greatest saint will be the poorest, the most trusting. It is not the poorest one in and of itself, it is the poorest one who gazes at God and hopes in God (UD June 10, 1959).

What is trust? It is hope completely impregnated with love. We hope because we love: there you have trust, trust that expresses itself not only through distinct acts but has created an attitude of soul (JVVD 837).

Hope can only grow through the progressive impoverishment of our whole being. This liberates our hope and leads us to trust.

What is this impoverishment? Is it a matter

of material goods? Let us remember that the rich young man "was *very* rich" (Lk 18:23). It was his attachment to his possessions that kept him from following Jesus. Poverty does not mean having nothing, admittedly; essentially it is not being attached to what we need. These material goods should not hold us back: "You cannot serve God and money" (Lk 16:13).

Spiritual poverty is an attitude of soul that we cannot reach by ourselves. It is God who unties the bonds that attach us to our riches. He is the One who really makes us poor and He is the one who comes when nothing within us stops His coming anymore. In our spiritual life, we would like to guide ourselves according to our own plans, do something for God as we understand it, earn "merits". During prayer, what quite often hinders us is a certain search for light, the desire to find God as we would like Him to be.

Now, most of the time what we experience is our failure, how impossible it is for us to raise ourselves up to God from where we are. We are unable to have a single "good thought", a single surge of love. The somewhat painful experience of our poverty is one of the first lights God gives us and this experience is inevitable. What is to be done? Think that we are not made for this and give up prayer? No! This is the time for waiting, for pure hope. "Without me you can do nothing" (Jn 15:6): this principle guides everyone's spiritual life; we need to be convinced of this. Learning to remain face to face with God having only the experience of our poverty is the effort we need to make. Our recourse to God then becomes more intense, more active.

It is a matter of knowing how to use our poverty; success in silent prayer is the success of poverty (UD June 10, 1959). We need to ask God to act according to what He is. He is mercy, self-diffusing love: such is God's Being. Love in Him is not a simple quality. If we are truly poor in front of Him, then He will invade us. True poverty can only be trusting because it is the experience of mercy; without trust – *hope completely impregnated with love* – it would be unbearable.

> My God, in my poverty I want to love You.
> I am seeking You. See Your child.
> I ask You, my God,
> to follow the movement of Your paternal love,
> and to come all the way to me.
> Trusting, I await Your coming.

The great doctor of the virtue of hope is little Thérèse. She speaks of a little way… the way of love and trust (cf. LC July 17, 1897). She recommends standing in God's presence like a "little child" (cf. Ms B 4r), learning to make "receptacles of mercy" of our weaknesses and even our sins, and she invites us to "trust blindly" in divine mercy.

She explains that she wanted "to find an elevator to get up to Jesus" and the elevator she found was "the arms of Jesus"! Only God's strength can carry us to Him! But while waiting for the elevator to come, we need to be patient and not remain passive. Thérèse stayed at the bottom of the stairs that she could not climb by herself; she called to Jesus while "lifting her little foot," and God came down and carried her up to Him.

This attitude found in the Gospel is very pure, very simple and very demanding: leave pride of place to God's action, surrender yourself.… Trusting so much it made her audacious, Thérèse affirmed: "We can never have too much confidence in God who is so powerful and merciful. We obtain from Him as much as we hope for" (quoted by Father Marie-Eugène, UTL 111).

These words express the fruit of her life experience, lived in a constant relationship with God and in radiant charity in the heart of one of the darkest nights of faith lasting throughout the last year and a half before her death.

Jacques Fesch, a criminal condemned to death, returned to God in his prison. The night before his execution he wrote: "The execution will take place tomorrow.... Jesus is very near to me. He draws me closer and closer.... I wait in the dark, and in peace.... I await love" [*Light Over the Scaffold* (ST PAULS/Alba House, 1996), 108-109].

Poverty, when it is an experience of love, becomes a poverty that is loved, however painful it may be. We are all prodigal sons, and in whatever abyss of misery we may be, there is always an abyss of mercy that opens before us if we call for it. However far away we may be, Jesus will come and find us. This invincible trust in God is the source of all peace.

Blessed is the tax collector in the parable whose humble prayer touched God's heart (Lk 18:9-14).

"Blessed are the poor in spirit..." (Mt 5:3).

TWELFTH DAY

COME DAY, COME NIGHT

Whether it is night ... whether it is day, the seed develops (see Mk 4:26–29).

This little parable highlights the seed's strength, its life. The seed contains life within; it is alive, it develops.... How powerful is grace within us! The sower went on his way and, come day, come night, he trusted the life within the seed.

The seed's life goes on deep underground; it is independent from outside events. The weather conditions, storms, sun, all of that fosters the plant's growth. We are afraid of rain, and rain is necessary for it. We are afraid of the sun with its burning rays and they contribute to the plant's growth, giving it inner strength, flourishing life.

The same is true of the Kingdom of God within us. Its growth takes place in the darkness of faith, during the night, as it does for the seed. The whole problem of grace, of spiritual growth is there, with all its mystery. This life, the highest there is, is in-

carnated in what is human; it is veiled by what is human and we do not see it. I see the night, the day, the exterior circumstances; I do not see its intimate life. It is veiled because it cannot be perceived by the senses, it is spiritual.

Let us trust grace; spiritual growth takes time. God is in charge of what happens. He is the plowman, the sower; He makes this life, His life, grow.

Let us believe in the strength of grace, let us believe in this call to holiness that does not come from us, from our capabilities but from the vitality of grace. Let us trust in the development of grace whatever happens: through the nights, events, and vicissitudes. Nothing is lost; the strength of this life continues to develop through the night.... Think of the leaves that seem to be dead on a stormy evening as if nature were grieving, and the following day we can feel a new vitality. The same thing happens during the nights which pass over the soul (UD July 24, 1944).

What is the Kingdom of God? It is the reign of God's life within us. Divine life, participation in God's very life that is given to us, is a spiritual life and is therefore mysterious, ineffable. We are in the presence of a reality that our human language cannot precisely express, so Jesus spoke of it in parables. He did not say: "The Kingdom of God is..." but "The Kingdom of God may be compared to...." It is "like...."

On the natural level, in a certain way life is already a mystery. The sower does not know how the seed he has planted grows. He can see that "the seed sprouts and grows, he does not know how. Of itself, the earth produces first the blade... then full-grown corn in the ear" (Mk 4:27–28).

Thus does grace develop even more mysteriously. It develops "like" the seed, because, like the seed, it bears within itself the principle of its growth. These dynamics of grace are indeed what the parable reported by Mark expresses. Just as the dynamics of life are contained within the seed that grows and bears fruit, so does divine life within us possess in itself the principle of its growth. *This grace is not something that lies in the corner of the soul; it is alive and wants to flourish* (UD July 23, 1944).

We are created to live in union with God, to grow in His love. Just as the grain of wheat's nature is to produce heads of wheat, so it is the nature of grace to lead the soul to divine union: "...as You, Father, are in me and I in You, may they also be one in us" (Jn 17:21). That is the destiny our grace has in store for us; that is its purpose. *God is our end; to reach Him is perfection* (JVVD 128). The Second Vatican Council reminds us that we are all called to holiness.

But we cannot see the development of grace; *divine life cannot be perceived by the senses.* Teresa of Avila in her book *The Interior Castle* does however indicate specific stages of spiritual growth. These are the castle's seven mansions or dwelling places, each marked by progress in union with God. These are successive transformations of the soul in her journey toward her deepest center, toward the castle's central dwelling place where God resides and where, when grace has totally conquered her, she will reach Him perfectly. As for John of the Cross, he speaks of degrees of love: "The more degrees of love the soul has, the more deeply she penetrates into God" (LF stanza 1:13).

However, while the experience of the mystics leads them to glimpse guideposts in the spiritual itinerary they lay out, they do nonetheless affirm that the journey takes place in darkness. These milestones, however luminous they may sometimes be, cannot possibly be pinned down the way tangible phenomena may be.

Teresa of Avila points this out in fact: there is always a certain instability experienced by the soul. While the soul does "grow ... and this is the truth, she does not however grow the way the body does" (L 15:12). This growth goes through ups and downs, moves back and forth, without any logic or regularity that can be deduced. For John of the Cross, these regions where the soul journeys are *regions without paths*; each soul makes its own way.

When Joan of Arc, interrogated by her judges, was asked "whether she knows whether she is in God's grace," she answered: "If I am not, may God place me there; if I am, may God keep me there!" This was an admirable response that sprang forth from the humility of her faith and her trust in God.

Father Marie-Eugène, by underlining the *living and complex development* of grace, brings us back to faith. For the soul is indeed journeying in the night of faith. God plants the seed and He is the One who makes it grow. While grace does possess within itself its dynamic principle, nonetheless it needs nourishment and God alone is its food. Let us go to the sources of divine life, to prayer and the sacraments. Let us especially go to the Eucharist, "bread of eternal Life" (Jn 6:35). Nothing can stop the dynamics of grace, except the obstacle of sin and the lack of trust. And if sometimes everything seems lost to us, that is the time, more than ever, *to trust grace*. God is faithful. "If we are unfaithful He remains faithful, for He cannot deny Himself" (2 Tm 2:13). Grace always remains what it is: sanctifying grace that sanctifies us by purifying us, "power at work within us, able to accomplish far more than all we can ask or imagine" (Eph 3:20). Let us offer ourselves up to God's infinite power.

> My God, I am the field You water
> after sowing the seed.
> Open my eyes and my heart
> to the marvels of Your love.
> May the hurricanes I will encounter
> never annihilate my trust.
> Like Saint Paul: of this I am sure…
> nothing will be able to separate me from
> Your love.

THIRTEENTH DAY

CHRIST BELONGS ENTIRELY TO US

"Jesus loved His own in the world and He loved them to the end.… He began to wash His disciples' feet" (Jn 13:1-15).

He wants to wash His disciples' feet. He feels this need to express the true state of His soul in front of His disciples, in front of us. He puts Himself at our feet; He makes the most humble gesture He can make. There we have an attitude of loving humility.… It is Jesus' attitude toward us. It is a true attitude; He made this gesture before His Passion; He is still making it.

During silent prayer, come back to that. Jesus is here, at our disposal, to purify us, to sanctify us. The Passion is transitory; here we have His fundamental attitude. There is something eloquent and moving in this state: it does not lower Our Lord; it makes Him greater. This is disconcerting for us. He is the servant of our souls, He surrenders Himself for us. He affirms the mission that God has given Him; this mission places Him at our disposal. He is given over to the Church, to each one of our souls. Let us never be afraid to call upon Him; thus do we have Him fulfill His role as Master, Christ, mediator. He serves us with this humility, this affectionate simplicity that He expressed in washing their feet. Here He is, on His knees, to serve us. This is how He began His Passion.

"Do you realize what I have done for you?" Christ bent over His disciples so that they in turn would wash the feet of their disciples. We become servants because what we have has been given to us for others (UD August 6, 1945).

Father Marie-Eugène lived with and in Christ. *"My soul is full of Our Lord...."* As a father and master, he pointed to Christ. He marked out this path that touches the infinite with broad perspectives as well as practical remarks. In *I Want to See God*, he lays out the itinerary:

Untiringly, keep your eyes fixed on Jesus.... The Wisdom of the Word will be manifested, in darkness or in delight.... The soul, stripped and completely impoverished, will need to share in the sorrowful mysteries of Christ, while waiting to participate in the triumph of His life within her (JVVD 79).

Christ's mystery, with its times of joy, its somber times, its times of hope, is fulfilled in the life of every Christian.

In Christ's prayer before His Passion, He made only one request: that they all be one with Him, as He and the Father are one. This unity is vital. Why? God became man and Savior of us all. We belong to Christ. Jesus loved us in all His gestures, in all His acts. Beyond the painful events of the Passion, God's powerful mercy manifested in Jesus may be seen. Nothing will ever be able to separate us from Him.

So Marie-Eugène looked at Him in the Gospel; every single feeling, every period of Christ's life interested him deeply: love avidly wants to know every detail: *Jesus, we have come to be near You… speak to us, tell us about Yourself.* He often spoke to Him like this. Jesus, this companion, this brother, the Son of God, lived a man's life: *Show us Your reactions. I want to be one of Your friends, I want to follow in Your footsteps. I want to love the way You do, using the same means as You* (C-88 335).

"Unless I wash you, you will have no inheritance with me." Let us allow this shepherd to lead us. He is disconcerting! We gave ourselves to Him, He took us, and… He has left us to our own devices! He is nowhere to be found. Shall we abandon Jesus? Never! Persevering in the darkness and when faced with absence leads us to finding Him more deeply for Himself, in His divine Person and His Wisdom that go beyond our own intelligence. We learn never to reduce Christ's soul to ours, but to enter into His. *We are in communion with Wisdom that blinds us; we have the impression that Our Lord has disappeared. No, He has not disappeared, but you yourself are becoming Christ* (UD February 20, 1951).

> Jesus, take my cry to make of it Your prayer;
> may Your cry become my prayer,
> may I not doubt You
> now that I am beginning to resemble You.

Jesus, make us understand.... Perhaps we need to be more attentive to Him, to accept His light on our poverties and what He is expecting of us: it is the time for faithfulness. At certain times Christ's light does shine for us. But afterwards? Afterwards, the light goes out. It is a call toward something which has not yet been fulfilled, and in order to fulfill it, we need faithfulness. We need to follow the light's call, and the light's call in darkness.

Night that opens up to light ... Christ gives back joy. He who is forgiveness takes the sinner's place. He who is love takes the beloved's place. The human person receives salvation; our "yes" makes us enter inside Christ's mystery and participate in His Redemption. "You also ought to wash each other's feet."

That happens in a simple manner,
immersed in life:
Christ no longer dies,
but His members suffer.
There are 50,000 ways
to make contact with Him,
in dryness, anxiety, boredom!
I unite myself to Christ.
I meet up with Him from time to time,
I offer Him my suffering.
Christ is within me, and I am Christ.
He lives in me by faith,
He takes on my suffering, whatever it is.
The person who surrenders to God for others
is alone, like Christ,
the others are sleeping, even Peter....
I am alone, but Christ is within me.
Jesus, what I desire
is a likeness to You in love.

Jesus is our whole prayer. In loving Him, we find His Body, the Church; we become passionate about the Church as we are about Him. Tirelessly we follow love's movement. Because we have given ourselves to Christ, with Him we give life to the world. The Christian who has become Christ lives something of the blessedness of Tabor and the suffering of Gethsemane at the same time. We don't choose joy or suffering, we choose everything. We receive Jesus as a whole, in all His mystery. *How could you want me not to be happy, however much I am suffering?* said Father Marie-Eugène. *This joy surprises everyone, it is normal* (UD February 10, 1967).

Jesus did not explain suffering, He took it upon Himself, along with death, to its very root which is sin. He freed us from it once and for all. Journeying in the night, the Christian is bolstered by the soft light that comes from Jesus' Face, and from the mystery of Life that pours forth from Him. *Jesus, I love You; it seems to me that I love You perfectly.* At the foot of the Cross, we also discover Mary, our mother. We know suffering is something bad, but from evil God draws good: the victory of the Risen One!

At this point, light shines on the path

like at dawn. Christ is carrying His ewe on His shoulders. The most beautiful gift we can give to God and to the world is to give Him a saint: ourselves. Why hesitate? Trusting Jesus is the greatest act of freedom. Humbly, may I journey toward this union which is not a union based on feeling, but a union of being through grace. The branch bears fruit abundantly.

> On the road
> in the infinite and enlivening gentleness
> of the Resurrection,
> Jesus, You make Yourself the Bread of Life.
> You grasp us
> by Your glorious and hidden Presence.
> What joy for You, what strength for us
> if this Bread became "daily Bread";
> if more each day
> we were hungry and thirsty for You;
> if, by the Holy Spirit, we became You.
> Yes, come, Lord Jesus.

FOURTEENTH DAY

SERVANT OF THE KINGDOM, SENT BY THE SPIRIT

If we want to be apostles, the first thing to do, is to become aware of the presence of the Holy Spirit in our souls so that He may be the master of our activity (UD August 23, 1953).

The apostle is a prayerful soul who prays with the Holy Spirit. We build up the Church by praying. If we do not know how to pray, we will build an edifice without cement!

In the undertakings of our apostolate, we are the collaborators of the Holy Spirit. Whether it is a matter of feeding the poor, giving a spiritual teaching or administering the sacraments, the Holy Spirit is interested in all these tasks. We are His collaborators: we need to place ourselves at His disposal. For the apostle, there is no work that is only human. Everything is linked to building the Church.

May the Holy Spirit show us how to be both audacious and uncomplicated in our contacts, in our *teaching. In the wounds we will have to bandage and heal, may He show us how good God is and make us accept the truth. May we know how to bear suffering with patience and love: exterior suffering, perhaps suffering from hatred, suffering from the sin that we see in the souls who are in contact with us. The apostle bears the weight of inner and sometimes exterior sin. Let us take advantage of all of that to fulfill the mission that God has given us, so that we can accomplish it in as broad a way as God wants us to. Let us not diminish it by lack of charity or generosity, or by narrowness. Let us offer ourselves up to the Holy Spirit, may He be the Master so that through us He may fulfill in the Church what He has planned from all eternity, what the Father expects from us* (UD August 21, 1952).

Whatever God the Father does, He does "through Jesus Christ, in the Holy Spirit." He is the One who carries out God's plan in the world.

Our cooperation is necessary, but God's action comes first. At the beginning of the spiritual life, we lead our own lives. At a given moment, God takes the initiative: it is the time for a profound discovery of Christ and the Church, His Body. We decide to journey at God's pace from then on. This is a turning point in our personal lives and good news for the world. The Spirit wants to work through us, within us. We need to let ourselves be carried off.

The Father, through Jesus, sends me; not with my own strength, but through His grace. This choice is a privilege of baptismal grace; it associates us with Christ's saving gesture: "At Your command, I will lower the nets." When should I begin? Today, as I am, go where He sends me. *The great treasure is to be taken over by the Holy Spirit, to be transformed by the Holy Spirit* (UD August 1966). He does not want to be only our guide, our light, our inspiration. He wants to be Everything, inspiring our will and our action. *What does He come to accomplish within us if not to enlighten us and work with us?* (UD July 1966).

"You do not know where it comes from or where it goes." He is infinite, He is movement, always active. He who calls us into the deepest part of ourselves, in the same movement sends us forth toward our brothers and sisters, into this world where grace is already at work: these two movements go together, it is the same love.

As a disciple and servant, I learn how to work in the Lord's field. It is not mine; I cannot say: "I'm taking this little field and I am going to cultivate it for the good Lord"! It is the Holy Spirit who builds the Church! As apostles, we place ourselves at His disposal. For we will be apostles inasmuch as we are taken over by God, as God is alive in our souls: then our gestures will be those of the Holy Spirit.

Such is the secret of any apostolate.

And God will find His joy in seeing that we are truly in the service of His love....

Needless to say, hard, creative, competent work is necessary; needless to say, stewardship is necessary. The Holy Spirit needs these. But Marie-Eugène saw the limits of our too human constructions. He would say to us with a touch of humor: *We see through our own glasses. Some plan seems very important, and we think our whole future lies therein! Ah! The dreams of our intelligence!* (UD May 16, 1959). *Whereas all that matters is flexibility, openness to the Holy Spirit* (UD May 30, 1966).

Events also provide indications. God's thought is alive, it develops. We need to be ready at any moment, for an awakened faith allows us to perceive the Holy Spirit's action in everything. *In my own life, I would head in one direction, I thought the road was straight, and then: Stop! I had to stop short, take a turn … you do know when it is the Holy Spirit who wants that! We need to trust Him absolutely. When He disconcerts you, you can hope in God's all-powerful love* (UD December 24, 1966).

As a servant, I discover that throughout the *chaos of divine germinations*, God's hand is always there. Never are we more sure of God's will than when a providential event forces us to do this or that. Difficulties are no reason to think that we have made a mistake.… We may not understand what is going on, but God does not have to explain everything to us! What appears to be a loss on the outside may become the source of a greater good.

In his notes during a personal retreat Father Marie-Eugène wrote:

The Holy Spirit is alive; He puts all things in their proper place.
Surrender to Him to be available,
with closed eyes,
without trying to see into the future.
Use all my strength to accomplish
my current duty in His light, in His will (1954).

Holy Spirit, create within me the bonds
  of intimacy
that I need, that I desire,

that You need to accomplish Your task.
May this breath of the Spirit of love enter
   within me,
possess me and vivify me,
as He vivifies the Church.
May this breath, the Holy Spirit,
make me fulfill my mission.

Such is true prayer, whose weight we do not know. It will descend down into those deep, far away, mysterious regions where we have not been but that we will see one day in Heaven.

Let us offer ourselves up to this Pentecost!

FIFTEENTH DAY

MARY, FAITHFUL TO THE LOVE THAT TOOK POSSESSION OF HER

Our Blessed Mother kept the Word of God and this Word was often mysterious.

She lived a child's simple faithfulness, and then came the tremendous shock of the Annunciation, her requested participation; she adhered to the Word of God that was proclaimed. The first thing Elizabeth would say was: Blessed are you because you believed in the Word of God. In believing, you received Him.

Her whole life was a life of faithfulness. She was faithful to God's thought and she lived it out. God's will was manifested to her; she followed God's will in its successive manifestations.

She needed to be flexible in order to follow the movements of Love, of souls, of her Son, the movement of the Holy Trinity, all the way to Calvary....

She was faithful to the Love that took possession of her (UD August 11, 1945).

Mary.

We have already met you along the way. God's love took possession of you, you belong to Him. Who better than you has been a witness to the mystery of the Father, of the Son, of the Holy Spirit? Who more than you has followed the movements of God's Love for us? Mother hidden in God's plan, we will never completely penetrate your mystery. But we can enter into a deeper and deeper intimacy with you by following you, by praying with you, by watching you pray.

Mary prayed with her whole people. How? Very simply, in God's light. She was nothing but the Father's child, turned toward Him. *Mary paid no attention to herself, her only preoccupation was to unite herself to God; this self-detachment, this purity, was what allowed God to pour Himself out within her* (VM 47): He chose her to be the Mother of God and our mother. And that did not hinder her from gracefully living the social life of an Israelite girl of no distinction.

Mary, I watch you. Your prayer reveals to me what prayer is: a movement of my whole being toward God, keeping nothing back. You are so simple, so discrete, so humble that there is almost nothing to be said about your life hidden in God. We are often restless, preoccupied with worries, loaded down with our pride, our weakness.... Mary, keep me beneath your cloak of peace. By your pure trust, purify my trust. This may be the best way to enter into your mystery: stay silent near you, with you listening to the Word in which your life rests.

And then came the surprise of the Annunciation. Mary recognized the source of the message; she gave her consent without any hesitation *in an immense act of faith that created in her the capacities necessary for receiving the Word* (VM 49). By believing, she received Him, she surrendered herself; that movement was inspired by the Holy Spirit.

From then on she bore the Word and her whole being was drawn toward Him. *She plunged within all the more vigorously as on the outside there was anxiety, the anxiety of suspicions that were growing and that she could sense. So she enveloped herself completely in God while waiting in faith* (VM 50). Mother of God, from that very moment she was our mother. In her prayer she carried Love's immense plan.

One day Jesus exclaimed: "Whoever does God's will is my brother and my sister and my mother" (Mk 3:35). Was He not then praising Mary, praising what she was in her joyful, painful, but absolute faithfulness to God's call? Yes, she was the person who listened to the Word, who by her faith received it and kept it in her body, her heart, her freedom, for us, siblings of Jesus, for me. In the crowd, *if anyone had asked who Jesus' greatest collaborator was, we might have heard: Peter is..., John is.... In reality, it was Mary, and no one could see that* (UD May 16, 1959).

Mary did not understand everything when it happened. But her whole life long she espoused the movement of the Spirit. She watched Jesus. She knew He was the Son of God and Savior. She followed Him. Everything was there. When it was time for the Passion, Jesus went up to Jerusalem; she had to follow Him. Her Mother's gaze had gazed into Christ's eyes when He was a child, a teenager, a man.... By faith and love she entered into the depths of the man of sorrows. *She offered up her Son and surrendered Him completely.... She surrendered herself* (VM 52). The undertaking seemed useless; why did she stay? She continued to hope. *You are alone, Mary ... and behold suddenly this solitude is filled ... with what? With a strong and living hope that is in your heart: the Holy Spirit is with you. You received the Word from Him. From Him and through Him you now receive the Total Christ. Mary, your motherhood is developing to the dimensions of the world, to the dimensions of Jesus' sacrifice* (VM 160). At Pentecost, at the dawn of the Church, Mary was there, praying in the midst of the apostles. Her faith, her hope, her heroic love preceded and bore their own testimony. Hidden in the heart of the Church, Mary cooperated in the fulfillment of the Promise.

Mary, looking at you is not enough for me. In the poverty of my prayer and my life, I can reach despair. Mother of mercy, I need to find refuge in you.

Father Marie-Eugène noted this fact based on experience: at certain times of sadness, of discouragement, Mary comes close to us by means of a kindness, a seemingly insignificant coincidence that makes us recognize her presence. In the darkness, Mary shows herself to be a mother, totally mother, nothing but mother, a mother who was made for her child's weakness.

> *Knowing that his Mother is there,*
> *watching over him in the night*
> *makes the child's heart glad,*
> *renews his strength, fortifies his hope,*
> *gives him light and peace* (JVVD 894).

There is a contemplative discovery of Mary that, like the contemplative discovery of God, takes place in a light which cannot be distinguished clearly. It is an obscure and yet definite experience of Mary's motherhood. This creates a filial movement that comes forth from the depths and leads to a life lived in Mary's presence. Jesus Son of God and son of Mary wants no other place for us than His and He has given us His Mother: "Behold, your mother" (Jn 19:27). God's mercy is complemented by Mary's tenderness.

On the evening of his ordination to the priesthood, Marie-Eugène wrote:

Mary, I owe you everything,
it is you who led me and made me what I am
(M 20).

This means that, a long time before, he had taken her "home with him" forever. When Providence led him to Notre-Dame de Vie, the mystery of God's Life that passes through Mary deepened. She is mother wherever He is Savior; the mother of all those within whom the Spirit pours out grace. By participating with Christ in the construction of the Church, we have also been given to participate in Mary's mystery, for the love received from God is made to give life by extending Mary's motherhood. Spiritual fruitfulness is born in the development of baptismal grace, in the power of the Almighty who covers us with His shadow. *Our Blessed Mother has chosen you. She has called you to extend her, so that like her you may give off light and life, so that you may resemble her as much as possible... distributing her grace everywhere* (UD October 7, 1961).

One day we discovered with astonishment her active and life-giving presence in this place, and we believed in it....

Close to you, Mary, I remain "devoted to prayer" (Ac 1:14), guided by Father Marie-Eugène.

> *Mary, be Mother to the utmost,*
> *Mother of Life, Mother of Mercy,*
> *of this life that comes down even upon misery*
> *in order to revivify it, in order to resurrect it*
>
> (VM 173).
>
> I entrust my grace to you, this mustard seed.
> It is small and weak, make it grow.
> You are my Mother,
> I know my prayer will be answered.

ST PAULS

This book was produced by ST PAULS/Alba House, the Society of St. Paul, an international religious congregation of priests and brothers dedicated to serving the Church through the communications media.

For information regarding this and associated ministries of the Pauline Family of Congregations, write to the Vocation Director, Society of St. Paul, 2187 Victory Blvd., Staten Island, New York 10314-6603. Phone (718) 982-5709; or E-mail: vocation@stpauls.us or check our internet site, www.vocationoffice.org